MESSAGE FROM THE DIRECTOR

Dear Residents:

The D. C. Emergency Management Agency (EMA) has primary responsibility for ensuring that the city is safe from hazards of all types. EMA promotes community-based emergency management through preparedness, prevention and partnership with District families, communities and businesses. You can help us better plan for emergencies by encouraging your friends and neighbors to prepare!

This Guide will assist you to reduce hazards, home injuries and help you to personally prepare for emergencies.

Sincerely,

Peter G. LaPorte
Director

Evacuation

The District Department of Transportation (DDOT) has placed numerous road signs throughout the city that mark the 14 primary outbound evacuation or event routes. There are also inbound routes for emergency vehicles. These routes are clearly marked with signage directing motorists either to I-495 or to the Mall. During an emergency, stay tuned to your local emergency station or listen to emergency personnel for instructions on which route to follow.

> The DCEMA website -- *http://dcema.dc.gov* -- contains preparedness information, including the District Response Plan (DRP) and other materials.
>
> The DDOT website -- *http://ddot.dc.gov* -- contains additional evacuation information.

Evacuation map

The map shown on the next page highlights the primary corridors radiating from downtown Washington, D.C. that have been identified as emergency event / evacuation routes (in red). Each of the routes extends to the Capital Beltway (I-495) and beyond.

During a major event or emergency situation, radial evacuation routes featuring traffic signals will be timed. In addition, 70 critical intersections on the event / evacuation routes within Washington, D.C. will be manned with uniformed police officers to expedite the flow of traffic and to prevent bottlenecks. These officers will also be able to direct you to alternate routes should an emergency warrent the closing of current event / evacuation routes.

> Pennsylvania Avenue, NW, between Rock Creek Park and the U.S. Capitol serves as the dividing line for event / evacuation routes. When evacuation is ordered, motorists north of Pennsylvania Avenue will be directed North, East, and West on radial event / evacuation routes; motorists south of Pennsylvania Avenue will be directed South, East, and West on radial event / evacuation routes. None of the routes cross and no vehicles will be permitted to cross Pennsylvania Avenue during an emergency evacuation.

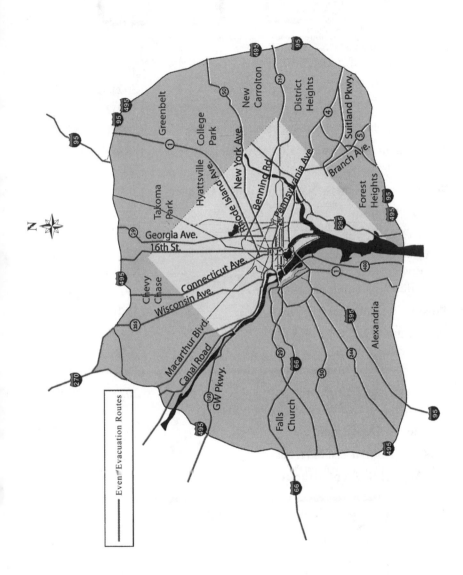

Washington D.C. Area

Important District Telephone Numbers
Police, Fire, & EMS

EMERGENCIES
911

NON-EMERGENCIES
311

311 is a toll-free phone number to request police services in
non-emergency situations. These are situations that are not
serious, not life threatening, or not currently in progress.

The Mayor's City-wide Call Center	(202) 727-1000
DC Emergency Management Agency **(24 hour)**	(202) 727-6161
(For the hearing impaired)	(202) 727-3323
Department of Mental Health	(888) 793-4357
(Access HelpLine)	(202) 561-7000
American Red Cross, National Capital Chapter	(202) 728-6401
Verizon **(phone)**	(800) 275-2355
PEPCO **(electric)**	
(Customer service)	(202) 833-7500
(Power outages)	(877) PEPCO-62
(Life-threatening emergencies)	(202) 872-3432
Poison Control Center	(800) 222-1222
Washington Gas	
(Customer service)	(202) 624-6049
(Natural Gas Emergency Number)	(703) 750-1400
DC Water and Sewer Authority	(202) 787-2000
(Water and Sewer Emergency Number)	(202) 612-3400
DC Health Department	(202) 442-5999
Pets and Animal Issues (Dept. of Health)	(202) 535-2323
DC Animal Shelter **(24-hours)**	(202) 576-6664

Additional information on emergency
preparedness is available by calling
FEMA at: (800) 480-2520, or
DC EMA at: (202) 727-6161

Or on the Internet at:
http://www.fema.gov
http://www.redcross.org
http://dcema.dc.gov

District of Columbia Emergency Management Agency
2000 14th Street N.W., 8th Floor Washington, DC 20009

IT'S

A

DISASTER!

...and what are <u>you</u> gonna do about it?

2nd Edition

A Basic First Aid & Disaster Preparedness Manual from FedHealth™

by Bill & Janet Liebsch

www.fedhealth.net or call 1-888-999-4325

Fedhealth
7739 E. Broadway Blvd. #416
Tucson, AZ 85710-3941
info@fedhealth.net

ISBN 1-930131-01-1
Published by Fedhealth
Indexing services by Michelle B. Graye, Tucson, AZ.
Printed by Central Plains Book Manufacturing • www.centralplainsbook.com
Printed on recycled paper
2nd Edition: May 2001 (Revised Nov 2002)

Library of Congress Catalog Card Number: 00-103061

This Manual is available through the following methods:

- for individual purchase directly from Fedhealth

- for schools, youth groups and other nonprofits to use as a fundraising project and earn 65% profits

- for companies and organizations to customize as giveaways for employees, customers, tradeshows, etc.

- for qualified Resellers to offer online and in stores!

For more information please visit Fedhealth online:

http://www.fedhealth.net

(Click on *BOOKS*, the *ULTIMATE FUNDRAISER*, *CORPORATE SALES*, or *RESELLER PROGRAM*)

ACKNOWLEDGEMENTS

We would like to personally thank the following individuals for their support and belief in us and in this venture over the past several years:

Stephen R. (Dex) Dexter, William H. (Bill) Holt of Sammamish, Washington, and Genevieve, Richard and Ann Worley.

We also would like to thank several individuals who contributed materials, expertise and time to help us during the compilation of this manual: Doug Abromeit (USFS National Avalanche Center), Peter Baker (American Red Cross), Jeff Brown (American Avalanche Association), Max London (OCIPEP), Rick Meitzler (Charleston County EPD), Joe & Tamara Melanson, Chris Tucker (OCIPEP), and various personnel from the Canadian Red Cross.

And most important of all…

Thank you to ALL our family members and friends who believed in us and supported us spiritually and emotionally!

ABOUT THE AUTHORS

Bill and Janet Liebsch are the original founders of Fedhealth, a publishing and marketing corporation formed to help the public focus on preparedness and health-related issues. They consider themselves "social entrepreneurs" dedicated to developing and marketing programs that primarily benefit schools and nonprofit organizations.

Fedhealth's series of Manuals will be expanded to include other languages plus other health, life preparedness and safety-related topics (e.g. aging, pregnancy, handicaps, etc.)

DISCLAIMER

The authors of this Manual are not licensed physicians, and the enclosed suggestions should not replace the medical advice of trained medical staff. This information is not intended as a substitute for a first aid course, but reviews some basic first aid measures that could be used when medical assistance is delayed or temporarily unavailable due to a major disaster or crisis.

DEDICATION

This manual is dedicated to Volunteers all around the world who give their heart, soul, energy, and time unselfishly for the betterment of our society. Thank you.

CONTENTS

SIDS ALLIANCE AWARENESS MESSAGE

FEDHEALTH AND THE SIDS ALLIANCE
...HELPING YOU PREPARE FOR LIFE!

Fedhealth and the Sudden Infant Death Syndrome (SIDS) Alliance are combining efforts to educate the public on safety and preparedness issues that involve the entire family.

Many people have asked "why the SIDS Alliance?" Since both Fedhealth and the SIDS Alliance focus on education, safety, and awareness it was a perfect opportunity to collaborate and heighten awareness about SIDS through our company's book.

Sudden Infant Death Syndrome is a medical disorder, which claims the lives of thousands of young children one day to one year of age. SIDS is the term used to describe infant deaths that remain unexplained after a thorough autopsy, death scene investigation and review of the medical history, ruling out other natural or unnatural causes of death.

Both Fedhealth and the SIDS Alliance want everyone to recognize that SIDS can strike without warning and affects families of all races and income levels.

"Fedhealth has taken a leadership role in the national promotion of SIDS awareness," said Kendra Davenport, Vice President of Development of the SIDS Alliance. "Through the sales of Fedhealth books, the Alliance, our Affiliates and everyone who buys or reads one of them benefits. It truly is a win-win effort!"

The SIDS Alliance is a national, not-for-profit voluntary health organization dedicated to the support of SIDS families, public education and medical research.

For more information about Sudden Infant Death Syndrome and the SIDS Alliance please visit www.sidsalliance.org or call 1-800-221-SIDS (7437).

FACTS & INFORMATION ABOUT
SUDDEN INFANT DEATH SYNDROME

Did you know...

... Sudden Infant Death Syndrome (SIDS) is the sudden and unexplained and unexpected death of an otherwise healthy infant under one year of age?!

... more children die of SIDS in a year than all children who die of cancer, heart disease, pneumonia, child abuse, AIDS, cystic fibrosis, and muscular dystrophy... combined?!

... **African-American** babies are almost **twice** as likely to die of SIDS than white babies?! ... and the rate of SIDS in the **Native-American** population is almost **3 times higher** than that of the population at large?!

... more babies die of SIDS during the cold weather months?!

... placing a baby on its back to sleep is best - doctors have found that a baby will NOT choke on spit-up or vomit so remember... "back is best"!

... since the "Back to Sleep Campaign" was announced in 1992 the SIDS rate has decreased by 42%... the equivalent of sparing the lives of 2,000 babies a year?!

... studies show *changing* a baby's sleeping position from his/her back can potentially increase the risk of SIDS **dramatically**?!

... After 30 years of research, scientists still have not found a cause for SIDS. Although there are factors that may reduce the risk of SIDS, there is no way to predict or prevent Sudden Infant Death Syndrome.

SIDS is not contagious.
SIDS is not caused by immunizations.
SIDS is not caused by child abuse.
SIDS is no one's fault.

SUDDEN INFANT DEATH SYNDROME (SIDS) ALLIANCE
Advancing Infant Safety and Survival Across America

The SIDS Alliance and Fedhealth are asking everyone to <u>PLEASE</u> educate child-care providers, baby-sitters, grandparents, and others about the SIDS risk reduction factors!

REDUCE THE RISKS FOR SIDS:
A CHECKLIST FOR NEW PARENTS

✓ Place your baby on the back to sleep at nighttime and naptime
✓ Use a firm mattress in a safety-approved crib
✓ Eliminate soft bedding from your baby's sleep area
✓ Keep your baby's face and head clear of blankets and other coverings during sleep
✓ Be careful not to overheat your baby
✓ Provide a smoke-free environment for your baby
✓ Educate baby sitters, child care providers and grandparents about SIDS risks
✓ And don't forget to enjoy your new baby!

HELP FIGHT SIDS WITH THIS CHECKLIST AND A CHECK
CALL 1-800-221-SIDS

NOTE: *While doctors are hopeful that following these recommendations will continue to save lives, it is important to keep in mind that faithful adherence will still not prevent all SIDS deaths. The tragic truth is that any baby may be vulnerable to SIDS despite their parents' best efforts. Therefore, it is imperative that we all continue to support scientific efforts to uncover other risk factors and possible causes in order to solve the SIDS puzzle for good.*

SIDS ALLIANCE ★ 1314 BEDFORD AVENUE, SUITE 210 ★ BALTIMORE, MARYLAND 21208

www.fedhealth.net or call 1-888-999-4325

SUDDEN INFANT DEATH SYNDROME (SIDS) ALLIANCE
Advancing Infant Safety and Survival Across America

The Sudden Infant Death Syndrome Alliance is a national, non-profit voluntary health organization uniting parents, caregivers, health professionals and researchers with government, business and community service groups concerned about the health of America's babies. The SIDS Alliance is a partner with the U.S. Public Health Service and the American Academy of Pediatrics in the Back to Sleep campaign, a nationwide infant health initiative aimed at reducing SIDS and infant mortality. The Back to Sleep campaign is responsible for reducing the rate of SIDS by 43% since 1992 - the equivalent of sparing the lives of 2,000 babies a year.

The SIDS Alliance funds medical research; offers emotional support nationally and through local Affiliate programs to families who have lost babies to SIDS; and supplies up-to-date information on SIDS to the general public, particularly new and expectant parents, through a nationwide, 24-hour toll free hotline **(1-800-221-7437)** and website **www.sidsalliance.org**.

SIDS ALLIANCE ★ 1314 BEDFORD AVENUE, SUITE 210 ★ BALTIMORE, MARYLAND 21208

INTRODUCTION

If you have never been involved in any type of major disaster, count yourself among the lucky ones and realize that disasters can happen anywhere and anytime!! As victims of disasters can confirm, the confusion immediately following a disaster is <u>scary</u> - especially if you have not prepared yourself in advance and discussed these ideas with your family members!

Hopefully every time you see or hear about a disaster it makes you stop and think... "What if that was me or my family?" But what have <u>YOU</u> done to get yourself and your family ready? The best thing you can do to deal with any type of disaster is...

<u>**BE AWARE**</u>... <u>**BE PREPARED**</u>... and... <u>**HAVE A PLAN**</u>!

If you do these 3 things, the life you save could be your own... because what you <u>don't</u> know <u>CAN</u> hurt you!

The more we [the public] are prepared for a disaster, the less strain we place on our local emergency services. Any major disaster will temporarily swamp the emergency service groups, therefore, both the Red Cross and the Federal Emergency Management Agency (FEMA) recommend persons to try to be self-sufficient for at least <u>72</u> HOURS following a disaster! And if you are prepared for a longer period... that's even better!

A majority of this information was compiled from various publications provided by the Red Cross, FEMA and Canada's OCIPEP to help assist you in preparing for various types of disasters and basic first aid. It also will offer many suggestions on personal checklists and important telephone numbers for your family members and emergency groups that can be written in the spaces provided or attached inside this Manual.

We realize you may not experience every type of disaster in your part of the world but if you ever travel away from home you could potentially be placed in a disaster situation so please educate yourself and your family.

Throughout this Manual, Fedhealth will mention products which may already be in your home to help you develop cost-effective solutions for you and your family! As a courtesy Fedhealth provides links through our web site to vendors who offer discounts and savings on some products mentioned here and other types of health and preparedness products.

Please stop your hectic lives for just a few hours and sit down with your family while reading this Manual to discuss how each of you would handle these types of situations.

It will be quality time with your loved ones and could save your lives!

Disaster Facts
&
Figures

DISASTER FACTS & FIGURES

Both natural and man-made disasters are becoming more common all around the world. The El Niño phenomenon impacted billions of people throughout the late 1990s followed by the cooling effects of La Niña between 1999 and 2001. Trends indicate a return of El Niño by mid-2002.

According to the National Oceanic and Atmospheric Administration (NOAA), the interaction between the surface of the ocean and the atmos- • phere in the tropical Pacific causes El Niño and La Niña. Changes in the ocean impact the atmosphere and climate patterns around the globe. In turn, changes in the atmosphere impact the ocean temperatures and currents. The system swings between warm (El Niño) to neutral (or cold La Niña) conditions on average every 3-4 years.[1]

Some key elements in the increasing numbers of worldwide disasters include:

- Global warming trends
- Larger cities are sprawling into high-risk zones
- World population is nearly 6 billion and growing causing global water consumption to increase
- Humans are damaging our natural resources (e.g. pollution, destroying rain forests, coral reefs, wetlands, etc.)

According to the United States Environmental Protection Agency, the earth's climate is predicted to change because human activities are altering the chemical composition of the atmosphere through the buildup of greenhouse gases - primarily carbon dioxide, methane, and nitrous oxide. The heat-trapping property of these gases is undisputed. Although the uncertainty exists about exactly how earth's climate responds to these gases, global temperatures are rising.[2]

The World Meteorological Organization/United Nations Environment Program Intergovernmental Panel on Climate Change also conclude that carbon dioxide is at record levels in the atmosphere and contributing to global warming.

The WMO also released evidence that the 1990s were the warmest decade globally since instrumental measurements started in the 1860s. So far 1998 was the warmest year on record and March 2002 was the warmest month on record further indicating temperatures are generally on the rise.

GENERAL FACTS & FIGURES ON DISASTERS

Without significant reductions in greenhouse gas emissions, scientists estimate the Earth's temperature and sea levels will rise, leading to increased flooding and drastic climate changes.[3]

The costs of weather-related disasters in just the United States alone average $1 billion per week!

Year after year it appears the most frequent natural disasters are windstorms and floods, which combined usually account for 80%-90% of the worldwide economic losses.

Every year hundreds of millions of people worldwide are evacuated or driven from their homes due to natural disasters.

According to Munich Reinsurance Company (a German company that monitors worldwide natural disasters) the following summarizes major losses <u>around the world</u>:

Year	Worldwide Economic Losses	# of Major Disasters	# of deaths by Major Disasters
2001	$36 billion (in US $)	700	25,000
2000	$30 billion (in US $)	850	10,000
1999	$100 billion (in US $)	755	75,000
1998	$92 billion (in US $)	700	50,000
1997	$30 billion (in US $)	538	13,000

Munich Re estimates that major disasters have ***TRIPLED*** since the 1960s!

Please note the worldwide losses in year 2000 seem less severe since most of the major disasters happened in less densely populated areas. However, the number of known deaths (14,000) from earthquakes in El Salvador and India in early 2001 was higher than the total number of disaster-related deaths throughout all of year 2000! This dramatic statistic proves how devastating disasters can be in highly populated areas.

FACTS & FIGURES BY TYPE OF DISASTER

Earthquakes
About 70 million people in 39 states are at <u>high</u> risk from earthquakes in the U.S.

Earthquakes can happen in virtually any region in Canada although most are concentrated in the western and eastern provinces and territories.

Over 600 million people around the world live in areas that are at risk from earthquakes.

Some of the strongest earthquakes in U.S. history (est 7.9-8.2) occurred on the New Madrid fault (general area between St. Louis and Memphis) back in 1811-1812. This area still experiences about 200 earthquakes a year.

Two of the most violent earthquakes in North America were in British Columbia's Queen Charlotte Island (8.3) and in Anchorage Alaska (9.2).

Thousands and thousands of earthquakes happen each year in Canada and the U.S. but most are too small to be felt.

Aftershocks may be felt for several days, weeks, months or even years depending on the force of a major earthquake.

Extreme Heat
Year 2000's drought was believed to be the most severe drought recorded in the past 100 years in many countries around the world.

Because men sweat more than women, men are more likely to suffer heat illness because they become dehydrated faster.

Storm windows can keep heat out of a house in the summer the same way they keep the cold out in the winter.

Fire
More forests burned in 1997 than at any time in recorded history. According to a report issued by the World Wide Fund for Nature, 80% of those fires were set deliberately to clear land for planting or development.

Over 80% of all fire deaths occur in places where people sleep - homes, apartments and condos, motels, hotels, and mobile homes.

FEMA reports over 84% of house and building fires are accidental while 16% are set on purpose.

Floods
The year 2000 floods in Mozambique made half a million people homeless and affected hundreds of thousands of people again in 2001.

More than 90% of declared disasters include flooding.

During a flood, 6 inches (15 cm) of moving water can knock people off their feet, and cars are easily swept away in 2 feet (.6 m) of moving water!

Flash floods can cause walls of water that can reach heights of 30 feet (9 m) or more.

Hailstorms

In 1991, Calgary Alberta experienced the worst hailstorm in Canadian history when a 30-minute storm caused about $400 million in damage!

On May 22, 1986 an unusual killer hailstorm in China's Sichuan Province left 9,000 people injured and 100 dead.

The largest known hailstone ever measured in the U.S. was found in Coffeyville, Kansas back in 1970 and weighed 1.67 pounds with a 17.5 inch (over 44 cm) circumference!

Hazardous Materials

As many as 500,000 products pose physical or health hazards and can be defined as "hazardous materials".

Each year about 400 million metric tons of hazardous wastes are generated worldwide.

There are about 38,000 hazardous materials waste sites in the U.S.

Each year, over 1,000 new synthetic chemicals are introduced.

In an average city of 100,000 residents, 23.5 tons of toilet bowl cleaner, 13.5 tons of liquid household cleaners, and 3.5 tons of motor oil are discharged into city drains each month!

Hurricanes, Cyclones & Typhoons

Japan, China, the Philippines and other parts of Southeast and East Asia average about 20 typhoons a year.

Over 75 million Americans live in hurricane areas.

An average of 5 hurricanes strike the U.S. each year.

Nine out of 10 hurricane deaths are due to storm surge (a rise in the sea level caused by strong winds). Storm surges can get up to 20 feet (6 m) high and 50 miles (80 km) wide!

One of the worst cyclone disasters in recorded history struck Bangladesh and India killing between 500,000 and 1 million people back in 1970.

Landslides, Mudflows & Avalanches
Flooding in Venezuela triggered landslides and mudflows that washed away entire villages and mountain slopes claiming more than 30,000 lives in 1999.

Peru experienced one of their worst landslide disasters when a 3-million-ton block of ice split from a melting glacier creating a destructive wave of ice, mud and rocks that traveled 10 miles (16 km) in just 7 minutes killing more than 4,000 people.

Statistics show there are about one million snow avalanches worldwide each year!

Nuclear Power Plants
The most immediate danger from an accident at a nuclear power plant is exposure to high levels of radiation.

Winds and weather could possibly impact people up to 200 miles (320 km) away from the accident site.

Special plans can be made to assist and care for persons who are medically disabled or handicapped within the 10-mile (16 km) radius of a nuclear power plant.

Terrorism
Before the September 11, 2001 attacks in New York and the Pentagon, most terrorist incidents in the U.S. have been bombing attacks, involving detonated and undetonated explosive devices, tear gas and pipe and fire bombs.

The Department of Defense estimates that as many as 26 nations may possess chemical agents and/or weapons and an additional 12 may be seeking to develop them. *(Per FEMA's data as of September 23, 2001)*

Thunderstorms & Lightning
On average, the U.S. has 100,000 thunderstorms each year.

At any given moment, nearly 1,800 thunderstorms can be in progress over the face of the earth!

It is a myth that lightning never strikes the same place twice. In fact, lightning often strikes the same site several times in the course of one storm.

Tornadoes
The U.S. has more tornadoes than any other place in the world and averages 1,000 tornado sightings each year.

In 1974, during a 21-hour period, 148 tornadoes ripped through 13 states and 1 province between Alabama and Ontario, Canada killing 315 people.

Tornadoes can produce wind speeds as high as 311 mph (500 km/h), move across the ground at speeds up to 75 mph (120 km/h), and reach as high as 40,000 feet (12,200 m) above ground!

Tsunamis
A tsunami (pronounced "soo-nam'ee") is a series of huge, destructive waves usually caused by an earthquake, volcanic eruption, landslide or meteorite.

A tsunami is NOT a tidal wave — it has nothing to do with the tides!

A tsunami can extend 100 miles (160 km) from crest to crest, build to heights of 100 feet (30 m) or more and move with speeds exceeding 600 miles per hour (965 km/h)!

Volcanoes
More than 65 active or potentially active volcanoes exist in the U.S. and over 40 of them are in Alaska!

According to the Catalog of Active Volcanoes published by the Smithsonian Institution there are about 850 active volcanoes that have erupted in the last few hundred years. About 600 of these volcanoes are part of the "Ring of Fire," a region that encircles the Pacific Ocean.

Volcanic eruptions can hurl hot rocks easily 20 miles (32 km) or more.

An erupting volcano can also trigger tsunamis, flash floods, earthquakes, rockfalls, landslides and mudflows.

Winter Storms / Extreme Cold
The leading cause of death during winter storms is from automobile or other transportation accidents

Cold weather puts an added strain on the heart. Exhaustion or heart attacks caused by overexertion (like shoveling snow or pushing a car) are the second most likely cause of winter storm-related deaths.

The risk of hypothermia is greatest among elderly persons who literally "freeze to death" in their own homes.

The Canadian ice storm of 1998 created an economic loss of almost $3 billion with massive power outages affecting over 4 million people!

Section 1

Family Information
&
Personal Checklists

Family Information & Phone Numbers

Place these records in a safe location (such as a metal box or a safety deposit box). We suggest you review/update the information several times a year to keep records current.

Since this information changes quite often, we suggest you use the information below as a guide and write the information on a piece of paper and paperclip it inside this Manual for easy access! Keep a record of each school your child/children attend every year. Please replace it every time there is a change or every new school year and make sure other family members get updates!

List work and/or school addresses & Phone numbers of all Family Members:

Parent/Guardian works at: _____

Work address: _____

Work Phone #: _____

Parent/Guardian works at: _____

Work address: _____

Work Phone #: _____

Brother/Sister works at: _____

Work address: _____

Work Phone #: _____

School information for each child in Family:

Child's name: _____

School name: _____

School address: _____

Main phone # for school: _____

Contact name at school: _____

- Will the school HOLD or RELEASE your child if there is an emergency or disaster?

- Where will the school move your child if there is an emergency or disaster?

Suggestion: Parents and Guardians may want to keep a copy of your child/children's information at your place of employment and with another family member in case of a disaster or emergency. Please make sure you update your records each year so everyone has the right data!

Other Important Family Information:

Please place these records in a safe location (such as a metal box or a safety deposit box). We suggest you review/update the information <u>several</u> times a year to keep records current.

Make a List of each Family Member's Social Security Number

Name: _____

Social Security #: _____

HMO/Insurance Policies:

Insurance Co. Name: _____

Policy #: _____ Telephone #: _____

Insurance Co. Name: _____

Policy #: _____ Telephone #: _____

Family Doctor _____

Family Doctor's Address _____

Phone #: _____

Closest Hospital Name _____

Closest Hospital Address _____

Phone #: _____

EMERGENCY PREPAREDNESS CHECKLIST

The next time disaster strikes, you may not have much time to act. PREPARE NOW for a sudden emergency and discuss these ideas with your family to create an **Emergency Plan**.

Even though this checklist looks long and scary, it is very easy to complete. We suggest you and your family members read this *entire* Manual before trying to sit down together since there are many tips mentioned here that will help you complete these checklists and plans!

PLEASE make some time in your busy lives to prepare for a disaster... a few minutes now could possibly save a life when a disaster hits!

Remember - be aware... be prepared... and have a plan!

CALL YOUR LOCAL OFFICE

(See Section 4 for phone numbers of State & Provincial Emergency Management offices and the Red Cross)

[ ] Find out which disasters could occur in your area.

[ ] Ask how to prepare for each disaster... if you still have questions after reading this Manual!

[ ] Ask how you will be warned of an emergency.

[ ] Learn your community's evacuation routes.

[ ] Ask about special assistance for elderly or disabled persons.

[ ] Ask your workplace about Emergency Plans.

[ ] Learn about emergency plans for your children's school(s) or day care center(s).

CREATE AN EMERGENCY PLAN

[ ] Meet with household members to talk about the dangers of fire, severe weather, earthquakes and other emergencies. Explain how to respond to each using the tips in this Manual.

[ ] Find the safe spots in your home for each type of disaster *(see Section 3 for explanations of each disaster)*

[ ] Talk about what to do when there are power outages and personal injuries.

[ ] Draw a floor plan of your home. Using a black or blue pen, show the location of doors, windows, stairways, and large furniture. Mark the location of emergency supplies *(see Section 3 - **Disaster Supplies Kit**)*, fire extinguishers, smoke detectors, collapsible ladders, First aid kits and utility shut-off points. Next, use a colored pen to draw a broken line charting at least two escape routes from each room.

[ ] Show family members how to turn off the water, gas and electricity at the main switches when necessary.

[ ] Post emergency telephone numbers near telephones.

[ ] Teach children how and when to call 911, police and fire departments *(see **Section 2**)*.

[ ] Make sure household members always turn on the radio for emergency information.

[ ] Pick one out-of-state and one local friend or relative for family members to call if separated during a disaster. (It is often easier to call out-of-state than within the affected area.)

[ ] Pick two emergency meeting places *(see **Emergency Plan**)*:
  1. A place near your home.
  2. A place outside your neighborhood in case you cannot go home after a disaster.

[ ] Teach children your contacts' phone numbers and emergency meeting places.

[ ] Take a basic first aid and CPR class. *(See **Section 2** for some Red Cross programs)*

[ ] Practice emergency evacuation drills with all household members at least two times each year.

[ ] Keep family records in a water- and fire-proof container. Consider keeping another set of records in a safety deposit box offsite.

[ ] Check if you have enough insurance coverage *(See **Section 3** for more information on flood insurance.)*

ADDITIONAL CHECKLIST FOR ELDERLY & DISABLED FAMILY MEMBERS:

[ ] Ask about special aid that may be available to you in an emergency for elderly and disabled family members. Find out if help is available for evacuation and in public shelters. Many communities ask people with a disability to register with the local fire department or emergency management office so help can be provided quickly in an emergency. Check if this option is available in YOUR community!!

[ ] Ask your children's teachers and caregivers about emergency plans for schools and day care centers.

[ ] If you currently have a personal care attendant from an agency, check to see if the agency will be providing services at another location if there is an evacuation.

[ ] Learn what to do for each type of emergency. For example, basements are not wheelchair-accessible so you should have alternate safe places for different types of disasters for disabled or elderly persons.

[ ] Learn what to do in case of power outages and personal injuries. Know how to connect or start a back-up power supply for essential medical equipment!

[ ] If someone in your home uses a wheelchair, make sure 2 exits are wheelchair-accessible in case one exit is blocked.

[ ] Consider getting a medical alert system that will allow you to call for help if you have trouble getting around.

[ ] Both elderly and disabled persons should wear a medical alert bracelet or necklace at all times if they have special needs.

[ ] Consider setting up a "Buddy" system with a roommate, neighbor or friend. Give this person a copy of your Emergency Plan and contact phone numbers and keep them updated of any changes. You may want to give this "buddy" an extra house key or tell them where one is available.

[ ] Consider gathering a few personal items in a lightweight drawstring bag (including a whistle, some medications, a small flashlight, extra hearing aid batteries, etc.) and tie it to your wheelchair or walker for emergencies. Make sure you rotate the items in the bag to keep them current and working!

ADDITIONAL CHECKLIST FOR PETS OR LIVESTOCK:

PETS:
[ ] If you have to evacuate your home, DO NOT leave your pets behind! Make sure you have a secure pet carrier, leash or harness so if it panics, it can't run away.

[ ] For public health reasons, many emergency shelters cannot accept pets. Find out which motels and hotels in your area allow pets well in advance of needing them. Include your local animal shelter's number on your contact number page *(See next section on Emergency Plan Contact Numbers)* since they may be able to provide information during a disaster.

[ ] Make sure identification tags are up to date and securely fastened to your pet's collar.

LIVESTOCK:
[ ] Evacuate livestock whenever possible. Arrangements for evacuation, including routes and host sites, should be made in advance. Alternate routes should be mapped out as a backup.

[ ] The evacuation site should have food, water, veterinary care, handling equipment and facilities.

[ ] Trucks, trailers, and other vehicles for transporting livestock should be available along with experienced handlers and drivers to transport them.

[ ] If evacuation is not possible, a decision must be made whether to move large animals to available shelter or turn them outside. This decision should be determined based on the type of disaster and the soundness and location of the shelter or structure.

PREPARE A DISASTER SUPPLIES KIT

Both the Red Cross and FEMA recommend keeping enough supplies in your home to meet your family's needs for at *least* three days or longer!

This topic is covered in detail in **Section 3 - Disaster Preparedness**. Please review this section with family members while creating your **Emergency Plan** on the next page.

EMERGENCY PLAN CONTACT NUMBERS

(Post a copy of this information near the phone for easy access!)

Out-of-State Contact
Name _____
City _____
Telephone (Day) _____ (Evening) _____

Local Contact
Name _____
Telephone (Day) _____ (Evening) _____

Nearest Relative
Name _____
City _____
Telephone (Day) _____ (Evening) _____

Family Work Numbers
Father _____ Mother _____
Guardian _____

Emergency Telephone Numbers
In a life-threatening emergency, dial 911 or the local emergency medical services system number

Police Department _____
Fire Department _____
Hospital _____

Family Doctors
Name_____ Phone # _____
Name_____ Phone # _____

Veterinarian: _____
Animal Shelter or Humane Society: _____

EMERGENCY PLAN, continued

In case you get separated from family members during an emergency or disaster, please decide on TWO Meeting Places or Areas where you can join each other. Please make sure your small children are included when making this decision and they understand why they should meet here.

Meeting Place or Meeting Area

1. Right outside your home _____

   _____

   (Example: meet by the curb or by the mailbox in front of home or building)

2. Away from the neighborhood, in case you cannot return home

   _____

   (Example: choose the home of a family friend or relative and fill in below)

   Address _____

   Telephone # _____

   Directions to this place _____

   _____

   _____

Section 2

Information
& Tips on
Basic First Aid

RED CROSS HEALTH & SAFETY PROGRAMS

For over 80 years, the American and Canadian Red Cross have trained tens of millions of people in first aid and CPR, translating the consensus of medical science into practical, easy-to-understand information for the public. These first aid and CPR programs are designed to enhance understanding and increase participants' confidence and skill retention.

AMERICAN RED CROSS HEALTH & SAFETY SERVICES

Some courses are available in both English and Spanish but please check with your Local Red Cross Chapter about availability of Spanish courses.

First Aid for the community:
- Basic Aid Training (B.A.T.) *for ages 8-12*
- Community First Aid and Safety
- First Aid for Children Today (F.A.C.T.) *for ages 5-8*
- First Aid - Responding to Emergencies
- Pet First Aid
- Sport Safety Training

Caregiving & Babysitting (Babysitter's Training, Child Care Course, Foundations for Caregiving)

HIV/AIDS Education (Basic, African American, Hispanic, Workplace)

Living Well/Living Safely (Lifeline: Personal Emergency Response Svc)

Swimming & Lifeguarding (Children & Family, Swimming & Fitness, Lifeguard & Aquatic Safety Training)

Youth Programs (HIV/AIDS Programs for Youth, Aquatic Programs for Children & Families, Baby Sitter's Training Course, Youth Services)

For the Workplace:
Core courses like Standard First Aid, Adult CPR/AED, Preventing Disease Transmission, plus various work-related supplemental modules available

For Professional Rescuers:
Emergency Response, CPR, AED Training, Oxygen Administration, etc.

CANADIAN RED CROSS HEALTH & SAFETY PROGRAMS

<u>First Aid for the Community</u>:
- Babysitting Course
- Child Safe
- First Responder
- Vital Link Public
- Vital Link Workplace

<u>Abuse Prevention</u>
Youth Connect = Relationship Violence & Child Abuse, Educational Presentation Services for youth and community leaders.

<u>Homecare</u> *(Ontario and Atlantic provinces only!)*
HomePartners, HomeMakers

<u>Water Safety</u>
AquaAdults, AquaLeader, AquaQuest, AquaTots, OnBoard

Please contact your local Red Cross office in the U.S. or Canada for more information on these courses and to see which programs are available in your area! *(See pages 156 & 163 for contact information!)*

Or you can access more information on the Internet:

American Red Cross http://www.redcross.org
Click on Health & Safety Services

Canadian Red Cross http://www.redcross.ca

Please note: Courses listed here are from both Red Cross sites as of March 2001 and subject to change. Please contact your local office regarding availability!

What are <u>You</u> gonna do about...
AN EMERGENCY?

Everyone should know what to do in an emergency. You should know who to call and what care to provide. Providing care involves giving first aid until professional medical help arrives.

The Emergency Medical Services (EMS) is a network of police, fire and medical personnel, as well as other community resources. People can help EMS by reporting emergencies and helping out victims until EMS can arrive.

During a major disaster, EMS groups will become swamped so if the public is prepared to handle some types of emergencies then we can help some of the victims until EMS arrives.

Your role in the EMS system includes the following things:

> *BE AWARE...* realize that this is an emergency situation and you could be putting yourself in danger!

> *BE PREPARED...* to do something about it!

> *HAVE A PLAN!* Check **ABCs**, Call 9-1-1 (or call for an ambulance) and help the victim, if possible.

TIPS ON MAKING <u>YOUR</u> "EMERGENCY ACTION" PLAN

1. *<u>BE AWARE</u>...* make sure it is <u>safe</u> to approach the area and the victim.

Use your senses...

> <u>Listen</u> for cries for help; screams; moans; explosions; breaking glass; crashing metal; gunshots; high winds; popping, humming or buzzing noises, etc.

> <u>Look</u> for broken glass; an open medicine cabinet; an overturned pot or pan; an open container or bottle near the victim; smoke; fire; downed power lines, etc.

Smell smoke; strong odors or vapors (leave if odor is too strong!), etc.

Look for signs - trouble breathing; trouble talking; grabbing at throat or chest; pale or blue color in face, lips or ears, etc.

2. *BE PREPARED*... the best thing you can do is **STAY CALM...** and THINK before you act!

Any time there is an emergency or disaster, most people are scared or confused and many do not know what to do. Take a few seconds and breathe deeply to help slow down your heartbeat and to calm down. Always ask if you can help... either ask the victim (if possible) or the people around who may be helping!

3. *HAVE A PLAN!* Check **ABCs**, call 9-1-1 and help victim, if possible.

...check the victims' **ABCs... Airway, Breathing, Circulation** *(see Tips on ABCs)*

...call 9-1-1, 0 for an Operator or your local emergency number for an ambulance *(see Tips on Calling for an Ambulance)*

...help the victim, if possible

...and STAY with the victim until help arrives.

Also, before giving first aid, you must have the victim's permission. Tell them who you are, how much training you have had, and how you plan to help. Do not give care to someone who refuses it - unless they are unable to respond!

TIPS ON THE ABCs...
AIRWAY, BREATHING & CIRCULATION

In an emergency, you need to check the victim for **ABCs**:

Airway.　　Open the Airway by tilting the head and gently lifting the jaw.

Breathing. Place your ear over victim's mouth and nose. Look at the chest, listen, and feel for breathing for 3 to 5 seconds.

Circulation. Check for a pulse using your <u>fingertips</u> (not your thumb!) in the soft spot between the throat and the muscle on the side of the neck for 5-10 seconds.

TIPS ON CALLING FOR AN AMBULANCE

Whenever there is an emergency, you should use the following tips to help decide if you should call 9-1-1 (or your local emergency number) for an ambulance.

<u>Call if victim...</u>

...is trapped
...is not responding or is passed out
...is bleeding really bad or bleeding cannot be stopped
...has a cut or wound so bad and deep that you can see the bone or
    muscles
...has a body part missing or is torn away
...has pain below the rib cage that does not go away
...is puking, peeing or pooping blood (called passing blood)
...is breathing weird or is having trouble breathing
...seems to have hurt their head, neck or back
...is jerking uncontrollably (called having a seizure)
...has broken bones and cannot be moved carefully
...acts like they have had a heart attack (chest pain or pressure)

<u>When you talk to 9-1-1 or the emergency number...</u>

...try to stay CALM!

...try to describe what happened and what is wrong with the victim

...give the location of the emergency and phone number of where
   you are calling from

...follow their instructions in case they tell you what to do for the victim.

Tips On First Aid and Spreading Germs Or Diseases

Whenever you perform first aid on anyone, there is always a chance of spreading germs or diseases between yourself and the victim. These steps should be followed no matter what kind of first aid is being done... from very minor scrapes to major emergencies!

BE AWARE...

> ...try to avoid body fluids like blood or urine
> ...cover any open cuts or wounds you have on your body since they are doorways for germs!

BE PREPARED...

> ...wash your hands with soap <u>and</u> water <u>before</u> and <u>after</u> giving first aid
> ...have a first aid kit handy, if possible
> ...put something between yourself and the victim's body fluids, if possible
>> <u>blood or urine</u> - wear disposable gloves or use a clean dry cloth
>> <u>saliva or spittle</u> – use a disposable Face Shield during Rescue Breathing
> ...clean up the area with household bleach to kill germs

... and... HAVE A PLAN!

> *...see TIPS ON MAKING <u>YOUR</u> "EMERGENCY ACTION" PLAN.*

Tips On Good Samaritan Laws

The definition of a "Samaritan" is a charitable or helpful person. Most states have Good Samaritan laws that were designed to protect citizens who try to help injured victims with emergency care.

If a citizen uses logical or rational actions while making wise or careful decisions during an emergency situation then they can be protected from being sued.

To learn more about your state's Good Samaritan laws, check with your local library or contact an attorney.

What are <u>YOU</u> gonna do about...
BITES & STINGS?

ANIMAL & HUMAN BITES

Americans suffer from approximately 2-3 million bites each year (mostly from dogs). Both humans and animals carry bacteria and viruses in their mouths, however, human bites are more dangerous and infection-prone because people seem to have more reactions to the human bacteria.

Things to watch for...
> **Puncture or bite marks**
> **Bleeding**
> **Infection** - Pain or tenderness, redness, heat, or swelling; pus; red streaks
> **Allergic Reaction** - Feeling ill, dizzy or having trouble breathing

What to do...
- Wash the bite as soon as possible to remove saliva and dirt from the bite wound - use running water and soap or rinse area with hydrogen peroxide
- Dry the bite wound by patting gently with a clean cloth
- Control any bleeding using direct pressure with a clean cloth or gauze
- Gently apply an antibiotic gel or cream, if available
- Cover with a sterile bandage or gauze, or clean cloth
- Call local emergency number or contact your Animal Control* (usually listed in the blue Government pages in phone book under County / Municipality)
- Watch for any allergic reactions for a few days (see list above)

...also...
- Get to a doctor or hospital if bleeding is really bad, if you think the animal could have rabies, or if stitches are required!

* Note: For Human bites, there is no need to call animal control, however, most states/provinces <u>do</u> require that all animal and human bites be reported to local police or health authorities!

INSECT BITES & STINGS

Things to watch for...
> **Stinger**
> **Puncture or bite mark**
> **Burning pain or Swelling**
> **Allergic Reaction -** Pain, itching, hives, redness or
> discoloration at the site; trouble breathing; signs of shock
> (pale, cold, drowsy, etc.)

What to do...
- Remove stinger by scraping it away with a credit card, long finger-nail or using tweezers. Do not try to squeeze it out since this will cause more venom to get in the victim.
- Wash bite wound with soap and water or rinse with hydrogen peroxide
- Cover with a sterile bandage or gauze, or clean cloth
- Place a cold pack on the bandage (a baggie or cloth with ice will work fine)
- Watch for any allergic reactions for a few days (see list above)

To relieve pain from a insect sting or bite:

Baking Soda - Make a paste of 3 parts baking soda + 1 part warm water and apply to the sting site for 15-20 minutes.

Meat tenderizer - Mixing meat tenderizer (check to see if it contains an ingredient called "papain") with warm water and applying to the sting will help breakdown the insect venom. (Papain is a natural enzyme derived from papaya.)

Clay mudpack - If outdoors in the wilderness, put a mudpack over the injury and cover with a bandage or handkerchief. The mudpack must be a mix of clay-containing soil since the clay is the key element.

Activated charcoal - empty 2-3 capsules into a container and add a small amount of warm water to make a paste. Dab the paste on the sting site and cover with gauze or plastic to keep it moist. (Note: the powder makes a black mess but it's easily wiped off with a towel!) This will help draw out the venom and it will collect on your skin. *(See TIPS ON FIRST AID KITS for more information on this product.)*

Urine (Pee) - Another remedy useful in the wilderness which sounds totally gross… but has a history of medical applications in a number of cultures… is <u>urine</u>, which will reduce the stinging pain. (Unless you have a urine infection, the urine will be sterile and at the least won't do any harm.)

Some potential pain-relieving and anti-inflammatory remedies include:

>**fresh aloe** - break open a leaf or use 96-100% pure aloe gel
>**vitamin E** - oil from a bottle or break open a few gel capsules
>**lemon juice** - from a fresh lemon
>**vitamin C** - make paste with 3 crushed tablets + drops of warm water
>**Store brands** - If over-the-counter methods are preferred, use a
>   calamine cream or lotion and aspirin or acetaminophen.

SEA CRITTER STINGS

There are too many types of sea critters in our seas and oceans and we cannot cover all the various types of stings and bites that could happen, however, some of the most common ones are shown below. If you want to learn more about specific types of sea critters (or marine life) then check with your local library or on the Internet!

Things to watch for…
>**Puncture marks or tentacles on the skin**
>**Pain or burning**
>**Swelling or red marks**
>**Possible Allergic Reaction -** Pain, itching, hives, redness or
>discoloration at the site; trouble breathing; signs of shock
>(pale, cold, drowsy, etc.)

What to do…
- Rinse the skin - use seawater, vinegar, ammonia, or alcohol (in whatever form is handy - either rubbing alcohol or liquor!) Fresh water might make it hurt worse!
- DO NOT rub the skin - it could make it worse!
- Try to remove any tentacles attached to the skin, if possible… but DO NOT use your bare hands… use a towel, gloves or tweezers!
- Soak the sting or make a paste (see p. 29) to help relieve the pain:
  For a tropical jellyfish - soak area in vinegar
  For a stingray or stonefish - soak area in hot water (not scalding!)

- Cover the sting with a sterile bandage or gauze, or clean cloth
- Call local emergency number, if necessary

To relieve pain from a sea critter sting:

Baking Soda Paste - Make a paste of 3 parts baking soda plus 1 part warm water and apply to the sting site until it dries. Scrape off paste with a knife or credit card to help remove some of the skin. (Note: two other quick and easy pastes are **sand and seawater** or **flour and seawater**! Scrape these pastes off using suggestions above.)

Urine (Pee) – Again, we know this sounds totally gross and weird… but urine (pee) does have a history of medical applications in a number of cultures… and will reduce the stinging pain. (Unless you have a urine infection, the urine will be sterile and at the least won't do any harm!)

SNAKE BITES
Poisonous snakes have triangular heads, slit-like pupils, and long fangs which make puncture wounds at the end of each row of teeth. Non-poisonous snakes will leave teeth marks but will not have the puncture wounds at the end of each row. According to the American Association of Poison Control Centers snakes bite over 50,000 Americans each year and Florida, Georgia, Texas and California have the highest averages. The biggest majority of these bites are from non-venomous snakes.

Things to watch for…
> **Puncture and/or bite marks**
> **Pain and Swelling**
> **Nausea and puking**
> **Difficulty breathing or swallowing**
> **Possible Allergic reaction** – Weakness, redness or discoloration at the site; trouble breathing; signs of shock (pale, cold, drowsy, etc.)

What to do…
- If possible, try to identify the type of snake but don't put yourself in danger!
- Wash the bite wound with soap and water.
- Apply a cold pack (a baggie or cloth with ice will work)
- Get to a doctor or hospital to receive antivenin
- Call local emergency number or animal control, if necessary

If bite is from a <u>Poisonous</u> snake, also do this...

- Remove constrictive items (rings or bracelets) since swelling may occur.
- Keep victim as still as possible to slow down circulation of venom.
- DO NOT apply tourniquet or ice - no longer considered helpful!
- Keep the bitten body part (hand, etc.) below heart level, if possible.
- Monitor breathing and make sure airway is open
- DO NOT let victim eat or drink anything or take any medication since it could interfere with emergency treatment!
- If possible and safe, remove venom - especially if help is hours away! (Most snakebite kits have proper venom extractors in them.)
- DO NOT use the "cut and suck" method... this can cause infection!

The worst effects are not felt for several hours after a bite from most poisonous North American snakes and it is best if the antivenin is given within 12-24 hours of the bite.

LAST RESORT - USE CAUTION SINCE... #1 - IT IS NOT CLINI-CALLY PROVEN AND #2 – IT AIN'T GONNA BE FUN!

This last option should <u>only</u> be used in an extreme case (if the victim is out in the middle of nowhere and there is NO way of getting professional medical attention within 24 hours) since it IS dangerous! This method is still being researched but is being used by Native South Americans:

When bitten by a venomous snake with <u>NO</u> chance of professional medical care <u>within 24 hours</u>:

- zap the bite with electric shock (touch the site with the wire disconnected from the spark plug and turn the engine over - this could be done with a car, outboard motor, 4-wheeler or motorcycle... or use a small stun gun)
- it appears the 20,000 volt pulse neutralizes the toxic effects possibly by altering the molecules of the venom
- cover the wound and seek medical attention as quickly as possible!

SPIDER BITES & SCORPION STINGS

There are only a dozen or so spiders that can actually cause symptoms or side effects to humans with a bite and the most serious are black widows and brown recluses. Tarantulas are also a little serious but do not cause extreme reactions and rarely will kill a human.

Scorpions will sting anything that touches them and their sting feels like a small electrical shock (almost like a hot needle). Scorpions whip their tails over their body and zap their enemy many times but it happens so quick it may only feel like one sting! The main threat of both spiders and scorpions is the allergic reaction humans have to their bite or sting so symptoms need to be watched carefully.

Things to watch for...
> **Bite or sting mark**
> **Pain or burning feeling**
> **Redness or Swelling**
> **Stomach pain or puking**
> **Fever, Dizziness or Headaches**
> **Difficulty breathing or swallowing**
> **Change in skin color or bruising** (looks kind of like a
> bulls-eye)
> **Possible Allergic reactions** - trouble breathing; signs of
> shock (pale, cold, etc.)

What to do...
- If possible, try to identify the type of spider or scorpion, but don't put yourself in danger!
- Wash the bite wound with soap and water or with rubbing alcohol
- Apply a cold pack (a baggie or cloth with ice will work)
- Get to a doctor or hospital to receive antivenin (if poisonous spider or scorpion)
- Call local emergency number, if necessary
- Watch for any allergic reactions or infections for several days

To relieve pain from a spider bite or scorpion sting:

Ammonia -- Place a small amount of ammonia on a cotton ball and apply directly on the bite or sting for a few seconds. This should help reduce the stinging pain, but please continue to watch for allergic reactions

Tea Tree Oil -- Apply a few drops of 100% Melaleuca alternifolia (Tea Tree oil) directly on the bite or sting but please avoid getting it in or near your eyes. This should help reduce the stinging pain but please continue to watch for allergic reactions.

What are <u>YOU</u> gonna do about...
BLEEDING?

CONTROLLING BLEEDING

Things to watch for...
>   **Source of bleeding**
>   **Pain and/or Swelling**
>   **Object sticking out or stuck in wound** (like a piece of metal or glass or a bullet)
>   **Shock** (pale, cold or clammy, drowsy, weak or rapid pulse, etc.)

What to do...
- Be aware of your surroundings and be prepared to call an ambulance (*see Tips on Calling for an Ambulance*)

If there IS an object sticking out of the wound (or possibly deep inside):
- Put thick soft pads around the object that is sticking out (or around wound)
- Gently try to apply pressure to help stop the bleeding
- DO NOT try to remove or press on the object!
- Carefully wrap with a roller bandage to hold the thick pads around the object
- Get medical attention immediately!

If there is NO object sticking out of the wound:
- Be careful since there might be something inside the wound that you can't see!
- Cover the wound with a clean cloth or sterile gauze pad and press firmly against the wound... and follow above steps if victim has an object <u>inside</u> the wound!
- If cloth or gauze becomes soaked with blood, do not remove it! Just keep adding new dressings on top of the old ones.
- You want to try and carefully raise or elevate the injured body part above the level of the victim's heart but be aware...there may be broken bones!
- Keep applying pressure on the dressings until the bleeding stops
- Use a firm roller bandage to cover the gauze or cloth dressings

www.fedhealth.net or call 1-888-999-4325

If bleeding won't stop:
- Put pressure on a nearby artery to help slow down the blood flow
  <u>Arm</u> – press the inside of the upper arm, between the shoulder and elbow
  <u>Leg</u> – press the area where the leg joins the front of the hip (groin)

NOSEBLEEDS

What to do...
- Pinch the soft part of the nose for about 10 minutes
- Have the person sit and lean forward
- Put an icepack or cold compress on the bridge of the nose

SLASHED OR SEVERED BODY PARTS/AMPUTATION

What to do...
- Keep direct pressure on the stump to stop the bleeding
- Find the body part, if possible, and wrap it in gauze or a clean cloth
- Put the body part in an airtight plastic bag, put the bag in ice water and take it to the hospital with the victim

What are <u>YOU</u> gonna do about...
BREATHING PROBLEMS?

ASTHMA ATTACK

Things to watch for...
> Noisy breathing or wheezing
> Difficulty in breathing or speaking
> Blueness of skin, lips and fingertips or nails

What to do...
- Make sure the victim has nothing in their mouth (keep an open airway)
- Have the victim sit up straight to make breathing easier
- If the victim has medication, or an inhaler, have them take it
- Try to keep the victim and yourself calm!
- If the attack is severe, call for an ambulance or emergency help

Some tips that could possibly help slow down an asthma attack:
(NOTE: These tips are NOT to be used as a replacement for medical attention but could be helpful in the early stages of an asthma attack.)

Pursed lip breathing - Breathe in deeply through the nose and out through your mouth with your lips pursed (like you are blowing up a balloon) at the first sign of the attack. It will help relax the body and possibly get rid of stale air in the lungs.

Drink a warm liquid or caffeine - Drinking one or two cups of coffee or tea that have caffeine could help relax the bronchial tubes. If you decide to drink a soda, do not use ice since the cold could possibly trigger an attack, so the warmer the better.

RESCUE BREATHING (NOT BREATHING)
Rescue breathing (or mouth-to-mouth resuscitation) should only be done when the victim is not breathing on his or her own. Make sure the victim is not choking on anything like vomit, blood or food *(if so, see **CHOKING**)* and check them using the **ABCs... Airway**, **Breathing**, and **Circulation**!

Things to watch for...
>**Grabbing at throat**
>**Cannot feel, see or hear any breaths**
>**Trouble breathing or talking**
>**Bluish color of skin, lips, fingertips or nails, and earlobes**

What to do...
- BE AWARE... make sure there is no head or neck injury first!
- Carefully move the victim so they are flat on their back.
- Tilt the head all the way back and lift chin. (Be careful with a child's or infant's head... just tilt head a little bit!)
- Look at the chest, listen, and feel for breathing for about 5 seconds

If victim is NOT breathing begin Rescue Breathing...
- Pinch victim's nose shut
- Open your mouth wide to make a tight seal around the person's mouth
- Give victim 2 slow breaths to make their chest rise. *(Note: For an infant, cover both mouth and nose with your mouth.)*
- Check for a pulse using your fingers in the soft spot between the throat and the muscle on the side of the neck for 5-10 seconds
- Continue Rescue Breathing if victim has a pulse but is not breathing...
  For Adults - give 1 breath every 5 seconds
  For a Child or Infant - give 1 breath every 3 seconds
- Check pulse and breathing every minute until the victim is breathing on their own.

...also...

- If the victim pukes... turn them gently on their side, wipe the mouth clean, turn them back and continue Rescue Breathing until they are breathing on their own.

NOTE: If victim is NOT breathing and DOES NOT have a pulse, see HEART EMERGENCIES for Tips on CPR!

What are <u>YOU</u> gonna do about...
BROKEN OR FRACTURED BONES?

A fracture is the same as a break and can range from a small chip to a bone that breaks through the skin. If you suspect a fracture, use a splint to keep the victim from moving too much and get professional help...and let the trained medical experts decide what is wrong!

NOTE: For Neck or Spine injuries, see HEAD, NECK OR SPINE INJURIES

Things to watch for...
> **Pain, bruising or swelling**
> **Bleeding**
> **Limb or area moves strange or looks strange**
> **Shock** (pale, cold or clammy, drowsy, weak or rapid pulse, etc.)

What to do...
- DO NOT move bone or try to straighten the limb if the bone breaks through skin!
- Try not to move the victim unless they are in danger
- Have the victim sit or lie down to rest the injured part
- If possible, raise or elevate the injured part
- Put a cold compress or ice pack on the injury to reduce swelling
- If help is delayed or you need to move the victim, splint the injury the same way it was found
- Be prepared to call an ambulance, if necessary

<u>TIPS ON SPLINTING</u>
A splint can be made using all kinds of items around the house like magazines, newspapers, a pillow, wood, etc.

Some basic tips on splinting include...

...always splint an injury the same way it was found

...make sure the item being used for the splint is longer than the broken bone

...use cloth strips, neck ties, thin rope, etc. for ties

...put something soft between the splint and the bone

...tie the splint <u>above</u> and <u>below</u> the break... but don't tie it too tight!

...touch an area below the splint and ask the victim if they can feel it... if not, loosen ties!

...put the cold compress or ice pack on the injury and keep the victim warm with a blanket or whatever is available.

What are <u>YOU</u> gonna do about...
BURNS?

Depending on how bad a burn is will determine what it is called:

First degree burns - hurts only the top layer of skin; turns pink or red; some pain and swelling; no blisters (usually from sun, chemicals or touching something hot)

Second degree burns - hurts the two upper layers of skin; very painful and causes swelling that lasts several days; blisters and possibly scars (usually from deep sunburn, chemicals, fire or hot liquid spills)

Third degree burns - hurts all skin layers and possibly tissue; charred, oozing or raw areas; destroys the cells that form new skin; nerve cells are destroyed and can take months to heal (usually from being exposed to fire or electrical shock for a long time). These types of burns can cause severe loss of fluids, shock, and death.

BURNS FROM FIRE OR HOT LIQUIDS

Things to watch for...
> **Skin is red and swollen**
> **Blisters that may open and ooze clear or yellowish fluid**
> **Minor to Severe Pain**

What to do...
- BE AWARE... and do not put yourself in danger!
- Stop the burning by putting out flames and move the victim from the source of the burn. (If victim is on fire, tell them to STOP, DROP and ROLL!)
- Cool the burn by using large amounts of <u>running</u> cool water for about 10 minutes. For hard to reach areas, wet a cloth, towel or sheet and carefully keep adding water!
- Try to remove any clothing, rings or jewelry in case of swelling (DO NOT remove any items that are stuck to the burned area!)
- Cover the burn with a sterile bandage or clean cloth. (Try to keep fingers and toes separated with the bandage or cloth, if possible.)
- Seek medical attention, if necessary.

Things you should NOT do...

- DO NOT break any blisters!
- DO NOT remove any item that sticks to the skin!
- DO NOT apply any creams, oils or lotions to the burns - wait for the medical experts!

CHEMICAL BURNS

Things to watch for...

> **Rash or blisters**
> **Trouble breathing**
> **Dizziness or headache**
> **Name of the chemical**

What to do...

- Rinse area with cool running water for at least 15 minutes
- Remove any clothing, rings or jewelry that may have the chemical on it.
- Make a note of chemical name to give the medical staff or hospital

ELECTRICAL BURNS

Things to watch for...

> **Electrical appliances or wires**
> **Downed power lines**
> **Sparks and/or crackling noises**
> **Victim may have muscle spasms or trembling**
> **Lightning during a storm**

What to do...

- BE AWARE... and do not put yourself in danger! If a power line is down, wait for the Fire Department or Power Company.
- DO NOT go near victim until the power is off! Once off, it is okay to touch the victim!
- Check **ABCs** if victim is passed out
- Do not move victim unless they are in danger.
- There should be 2 wounds - usually have both enter and exit burns

- DO NOT try to cool the burn with anything!
- Cover the burn with a dry sterile bandage or clean cloth
- Seek medical attention, if necessary

SUNBURN

Sunblocks and lotions should be applied at least 20 minutes <u>BEFORE</u> going in the sun so it can be absorbed into the skin layers. Remember… dark colors attract the sun and light or white colors reflect sunlight! And you can get sunburned on a cloudy day just as easily as a sunny day!

Things to watch out for…
    Blisters or bubbles on the skin
    Swelling or pain

What to do…
- Cool the burn by using cool cloths or pure aloe vera gel
- Get out of the sun or cover up so you won't get further damage
- Take care of blisters by loosely covering them and don't pick at them!

<u>To help relieve the pain from a sunburn if NO blisters exist:</u>

Baking soda - add ½ cup baking soda to a warm bath and soak for half an hour

Vinegar - put some regular or cider vinegar on a cloth and apply to sun-burned area.

Whole milk - apply a cool compress soaked in whole milk to the area.

Jing Wan Hong - (also known as Ching Wan Hung) an ointment that contains 8 Chinese herbs and is found in many natural foods and Oriental pharmacies.

What are <u>YOU</u> gonna do about...
CHOKING?

ATTENTION: There are two separate "**What to do...**" sections here... one for <u>ADULTS & CHILDREN</u> and a different one for <u>INFANTS</u>!

Things to watch for...
> **Trouble breathing**
> **Coughing or choking for several minutes**
> **Gripping the throat with one or both hands**
> **High-pitched wheezing**
> **Bluish color of skin, lips, fingertips or nails, and earlobes**

What to do... for <u>ADULTS & CHILDREN</u> *(see next page for INFANTS)*
- Tell the victim to try and cough it out
- If the victim stops breathing, then BE PREPARED to give the Heimlich maneuver and tell someone to call an ambulance.
- Stand behind the victim and place your fist (thumb side in) just above the victim's belly button
- Grab your fist with your other hand and give quick, upward thrusts into their stomach until the object is coughed up or the victim passes out.

If the <u>Adult or Child</u> passes out:
- Check for an object in the victim's mouth and try to clear it out with your fingers
- Begin Rescue Breathing *(see BREATHING PROBLEMS)*

If no air gets in <u>Adult or Child</u> during Rescue Breathing:
- Put the heel of one hand just above the victim's belly button and put your other hand on top of the first
- Give about 6-10 upward thrusts to try to clear their windpipe
- Check for an object in the victim's mouth and try to clear it out with your fingers
- Try to give Rescue Breathing again to see if air will go in
- Continue above steps until victim can breathe on their own or until help arrives

What to do... for <u>INFANTS</u>

- If the infant stops breathing, have someone to call an ambulance.
- Turn the infant facedown on your forearm and support their head with that hand
- Give 5 back blows between the infants' shoulder blades with the heel of your other hand
- Turn infant over so it is facing up on your forearm and use your first two fingers to find the center of the breastbone on infant's chest
- Give 5 thrusts to the chest using only 2 fingers!
- Repeat all steps until the object is coughed up or the infant passes out.

If the <u>Infant</u> passes out:

- Check for an object in the infant's mouth and try to clear it out with your fingers
- Begin Rescue Breathing (and remember... cover both mouth & nose on Infants!) *(see BREATHING PROBLEMS)*

If no air gets in <u>Infant</u> during Rescue Breathing:

- Continue above steps (back blows and thrusts on the chest) until infant can breathe on its own or until help arrives

What are <u>YOU</u> gonna do about...
COLD-RELATED ILLNESSES?

FROSTBITE

Frostbite (or frostnip which is the early stages of frostbite) is when certain parts of your body are exposed to severe or extreme cold - mainly your fingers, toes, ears, cheeks and nose. The freezing damages and dries out cell tissues and membranes, and extreme cases can impact deep nerves, muscles or even bones. (Some extreme cases can even lead to the loss of a limb!)

Things to watch for...
> **Skin appears white and waxy**
> **Numbness or no feeling in that area**
> **Possible blisters**

What to do...
- Handle the area gently; DO NOT rub the affected area
- Remove any constrictive clothing (gloves, boots, socks, etc.) and any jewelry
- Warm gently using body heat or soaking the area in warm water (between 100-105 degrees Fahrenheit / between 38-41 degrees Celsius) until area appears red and feels warm. *(Note: There will most likely be a burning sensation or pain as the area warms back up.)*
- Loosely bandage the area with dry, sterile dressing or cloth
- If fingers or toes are frostbitten, separate them with sterile gauze or clean cloth.
- Try not to break any blisters

Things you should NOT do...
- DO NOT rub or massage the area since this may cause damage to the cells!
- DO NOT rub snow on the area!
- DO NOT try to warm with dry radiant heat (meaning don't warm with a blow-dryer or hold in front of a fire or hot stove). Warm water is best!
- DO NOT try to thaw a frostbitten body part if it has a chance of re-freezing (if you are stuck in the wilderness) since this could cause more damage.

HYPOTHERMIA

Hypothermia can begin to set in when your body core (vital organs - heart, lungs, and kidneys) drops below 95 degrees Fahrenheit (35 degrees Celsius). When exposed to extreme cold for a long time, your brain begins to shut down certain bodily functions to save internal heat for the body core.

Things to watch for...
> **Shivering and numbness**
> **Confusion or dizziness**
> **Stumbling and weakness**
> **Slow or slurred speech**
> **Shock** (pale, cold or clammy, drowsy, weak or rapid pulse, etc.)

What to do...
- Gently move the victim to a warm place
- Check breathing and pulse (**ABCs**)
- Handle the victim gently and DO NOT rub the body or limbs
- Remove any wet clothing and replace with dry clothing and/or blankets
- If possible, place victim in a sleeping bag, especially if in the wilderness! (Note: Your body heat can help heat the victim... so cuddle up if the victim says it's okay!)
- Cover the head and neck with a hat or part of a blanket (75% of the body's heat is lost through the head)
- DO NOT WARM VICTIM TOO QUICKLY, such as putting them in warm water! (If the body warms too fast, it can dump the cold blood into the heart and body core causing a possible heart attack or a drop in body temperature.)
- If hot water bottles or hot packs are used, wrap them in a towel or blanket first and place them on the side of the chest or on the groin area. (If these are put on arms or legs then blood could be drawn away from the body core.)
- Let victim sip a warm, sweet, nonalcoholic drink.
- Closely watch the victim's **ABCs...Airway, Breathing, and Circulation**

Things you should NOT do...

- DO NOT rub or massage the victims limbs!
- DO NOT put victim in a hot bath! It will warm him/her TOO quickly!
- DO NOT put hot packs on arms or legs... put them against the body (chest or groin area)!

What are <u>YOU</u> gonna do about…
CONVULSION & SEIZURES?

CONVULSION
A convulsion is usually brought on by a high fever, poisoning, or injury and is basically like a seizure since the symptoms are similar.

SEIZURE
Seizures are usually related to epilepsy (also known as seizure disorder since seizures occur repeatedly during their life) and about 2 million Americans suffer from it. There are many types and forms of seizures that range from a short episode of blank staring to convulsions and most only last from 1-3 minutes or less.

Things to watch for…
> **Victim falls to floor and shakes or twitches in the arms, legs or body for a minute or longer**
> **Blank staring or vacant expression and minor twitching of the face or jerking of the hand** (usually a mild epileptic seizure)
> **No memory of what happened, confusion**

What to do…
- Have someone call for an ambulance, especially if victim was poisoned or injured or if seizure lasts more than 3-5 minutes
- Stay calm… you cannot stop the convulsion or seizure!
- DO NOT put anything between the victim's teeth or in their mouth!
- Move things that could hurt or fall on the victim
- Put something soft under the victim's head, if possible
- When the convulsion or seizure is over, help roll the victim on their side to keep an open airway.
- Look for any other injuries and keep checking **ABCs**.
- Stay with the victim until help arrives and try to calm them down

If victim is epileptic:
Ask if the victim takes any medications for seizures and help him/her take them according to the instructions.

What are <u>YOU</u> gonna do about…
DIZZINESS & FAINTING?

DIZZINESS
Dizziness is primarily a symptom and is usually combined with nausea, sweating, and a feeling of some kind of movement that really isn't there.

Things to watch for…
> **If dizzy feeling does not pass quickly or is really bad**
> **Fainting or passing out**
> **Vapors or strange smells**

What to do…
- Have the victim sit or lie down and close their eyes or focus on a nearby object that is not moving
- Tell the victim to try to keep their head still

FAINTING
Fainting is a temporary loss of consciousness and may indicate a more serious condition. It is usually caused because of a lack of oxygenated blood to the brain.

Things to watch for…
> **Visible injuries like bleeding from the ears or a bite or sting**
> **Pupils are enlarged or very small** (if different sizes, it could be a stroke)

What to do…
- If victim is still passed out, put victim on their side to keep an open airway.
- Once victim is awake, gently roll them onto their back
- Prop feet and lower legs up with pillows or something…if victim is not hurt
- Loosen any tight clothing, especially around the neck and waist
- Check **ABCs** (breathing & pulse)
- Make sure the victim rests before trying to get up
- If necessary, contact doctor if symptoms persist

What are <u>YOU</u> gonna do about...
DROWNING?

Things to watch for...
> **Signs of breathing**
> **Pulse**

What to do...
- Have someone call for an ambulance
- Once the victim is out of the water, check **ABCs** and see if there are any injuries or objects in the mouth
- If victim is not breathing or has no pulse, begin Rescue Breathing and/or CPR *(see **BREATHING PROBLEMS** for Rescue Breathing and **HEART PROBLEMS** for CPR)*
- Once victim begins breathing on their own, cover with a blanket or dry towels to keep warm and have them lay on their side for a while
- Stay with the victim at all times until medical help arrives

What are <u>YOU</u> gonna do about...
EYE INJURIES?

Things to watch for...
> **Severe pain**
> **Object stuck in the eye** (like a piece of metal or glass)
> **Redness and swelling**
> **Blurry vision or tears or trouble keeping eye open**
> **If injury is from a chemical, make a note of the name for**
> **Poison Control**

What to do...
- Avoid rubbing the eye since this can cause more damage
- Have the victim sit down with their head tilted backwards

If the injury is a <u>loose</u> foreign object:
- Wash YOUR hands before touching the victim's eye area!
- Gently separate the eyelids to see if you can locate the foreign object. You can try to remove the object by wiping gently with a moistened tissue.
- Ask the victim if they wear contact lenses, and if so, ask him/her to remove them.
- Flood the eye with lukewarm water or a saline solution
- Get medical help if you are not successful!

If there is an object sticking out of the eye:
- Put thick soft pads around the object that is sticking out
- DO NOT try to remove or press on the object!
- Carefully wrap with a roller bandage to hold the thick pads around the object
- Get medical attention immediately!

If the injury is from a chemical:
- Call your local Poison Control Center and be ready to tell them what the chemical is
- If victim is wearing contact lenses, ask him/her to remove them, if possible, to keep them from getting lost while flushing the eye... but ask Poison Control <u>before removing them</u>!

- Flush the eye with clean lukewarm water or a saline solution and make sure the head is turned so it doesn't pour into the other eye (if it is okay).
- DO NOT press or rub the eyes!
- Cover both eyes with clean dressing and bandage it firmly in place. (Covering both eyes will keep victim still!)
- Take victim to hospital or for professional medical assistance.

Things you should NOT do...
- DO NOT try to remove an object that is stuck into the eye!
- DO NOT try to remove their contacts (if any)... let the victim do it!
- DO NOT try to move the eyeball if it comes out of the socket!

What are <u>YOU</u> gonna do about...
HEAD, NECK OR SPINE INJURIES?

Things to watch for...

> **Convulsions or seizures**
> **Intense pain in the head, neck or back**
> **Bleeding from the head, ears or nose**
> **Blurry vision**
> **Tingling or loss of feeling in the hands, fingers, feet or toes**
> **Weird bumps on the head or down the spine**
> **Shock** (pale, cold or clammy, drowsy, weak or rapid pulse, etc.)

What to do...

- Do not try to move the victim unless they are in extreme danger and support the victim's head and neck during movement.

- Have someone call an ambulance immediately!

- Check to see if victim is alert and check **ABCs** (Airway, Breathing & Circulation) and if you have to give Rescue Breathing or CPR... DO NOT tilt their head back! *(see **BREATHING PROBLEMS** for Rescue Breathing and **HEART PROBLEMS** for CPR)*

- Try to control any bleeding using direct pressure *(see **BLEEDING**)*

- If the victim is passed out, hold their head between your hands while waiting for help to arrive. This will keep them from moving suddenly when they wake up.

What are <u>YOU</u> gonna do about...
HEART PROBLEMS?

<u>**Heart attacks**</u> can kill and most victims die within 2 hours of the first few symptoms! Most people deny they are having a heart attack even if they have chest pains and/or shortness of breath... but DON'T take any chances! These are your body's warning signs, so pay attention! A heart attack can lead to <u>Cardiac Arrest</u>.

<u>**Cardiac arrest**</u> means that the heart stops beating and causes the victim to pass out followed by no sign of breathing and no pulse.

Cardiopulmonary resuscitation (CPR) is used to help pump some blood through the body to the brain until the medical experts arrive! When you combine CPR and Rescue Breathing, you are giving the victim better odds of surviving since you help supply blood <u>and</u> oxygen to vital organs. However, if CPR is not done correctly, there is a chance of injuring the victim internally... especially on the elderly, children and infants!

If you have not been trained or do not feel comfortable doing Rescue Breathing please realize the primary step is doing the compressions to aid in the blood flow. It is not even necessary to stop and check for a pulse - just look and listen for signs and keep doing compressions! The Red Cross teaches many First Aid courses, including CPR, so please contact your local Chapter and ask about their courses! *(See **Red Cross Health & Safety Programs** at beginning of this section)*

<u>HEART ATTACK</u>

Things to watch for...
> **Chest pain that can spread to the shoulder, arm, or jaw**
> **Shortness of breath or trouble breathing**
> **Strange pulse (faster or slower than normal or sporadic)**
> **Pale or bluish skin color**

What to do...
- Tell the victim to stop what they are doing and sit down and rest
- Call for an ambulance immediately!
- Loosen any tight clothing, especially around neck and waist
- Ask the victim if they are taking any prescribed medicines for their

heart... and if they do, have them take it!
- Take a couple of pure aspirin, if available
- Closely watch the victim's breathing and be prepared to give CPR

CARDIAC ARREST (GIVING CPR) – Please be aware there are
steps below that include special instructions for CHILDREN or INFANTS!

Things to watch for...
> **Not responding or passed out**
> **Not breathing and no pulse**

What to do...
- Call for an ambulance immediately!
- Check **ABCs... Airway, Breathing, & Circulation**
- Tilt the head all the way back and lift chin. (Be careful with a child's or infant's head... just tilt head a little bit!)
- Look at the chest, listen, and feel for breathing for about 5 seconds

If victim is NOT breathing begin Rescue Breathing...
- Pinch victim's nose shut
- Open your mouth wide to make a tight seal around victim's mouth
  FOR INFANT - cover both mouth <u>and</u> nose with your mouth!
- Give victim 2 slow breaths to make their chest rise.
- Look at the chest, listen, and feel for breathing for a few seconds

To begin CPR
- Find hand position in center of chest over breastbone
  – see illustrations 2-1 through 2-3
  FOR <u>ADULTS</u> – *[see illustration 2-1 on page 54]*
  FOR <u>CHILDREN</u> – *[see illustration 2-2 on page 55]*
  FOR <u>INFANTS</u> – *[see illustration 2-3 on page 56]*

- Begin chest compressions using the following guidelines...
  <u>ADULTS</u> – Using **both** hands, compress chest 15 times
  in 10 seconds
  <u>CHILDREN</u> – Using **one hand**, compress chest 5 times
  in 3 seconds
  <u>INFANTS</u> – Using **2 fingers**, compress chest 5 times in 3 seconds

- Breathe into victim
  <u>ADULTS</u> – Give 2 slow breaths
  <u>CHILDREN & INFANTS</u> – Give 1 slow breath
- Repeat chest compressions and breathing until ambulance arrives!
- If victim recovers (starts breathing and pulse resumes), then turn victim onto their side to keep the airway open

CPR POSITION FOR ADULTS

Illustration 2-1

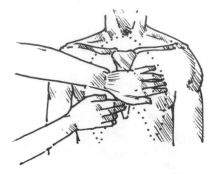

1. Find hand position

2. Position shoulders over hands. Compress chest 15 times.

CPR POSITION FOR CHILDREN

Illustration 2-2

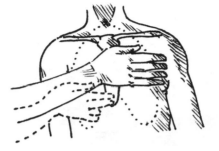

1. Find hand position

2. Position shoulder over hand. Compress chest 5 times.

CPR POSITION FOR INFANTS

Illustration 2-3

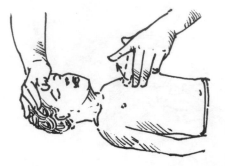

1. Find finger position

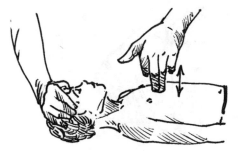

2. Position hand over fingers. Compress chest 5 times.

What are <u>YOU</u> gonna do about...
HEAT-RELATED ILLNESSES?

There are two major types of heat illness – Heat Exhaustion and Heat Stroke. Both are serious; however, **HEAT STROKE** is a <u>major</u> medical emergency and getting the victim's body temperature cooled down is more critical than getting fluids in their body!

Things to watch for...

<u>Heat exhaustion</u>
Cool, clammy, or pale skin
Light-headed or dizzy and weak
Racing heart
Sick to the stomach (nausea)
Very thirsty (sometimes)
Heavy sweating (sometimes)

<u>Heat Stroke</u>
Very hot and dry skin
Light-headed or dizzy
Confusion, drowsiness or fainting
Rapid breathing and rapid heartbeat
Passing out or slipping into a coma

What to do...
- Get victim to a cool or shady place (out of the sun) and rest
- Loosen clothing around waist and neck to improve circulation, and remove sweaty clothes
- Cool down the victim's body - put wet cloths on the victim's face, neck and skin and keep adding cool water to the cloth... or if out-doors, use a hose or stream. Also, fan the victim!
- Have the victim drink <u>cool water</u>! (NO alcoholic beverages – they dehydrate!)

If victim refuses water, pukes or starts to pass out:
- Call for an ambulance
- Put victim on their side to keep airway open
- Keep cooling down their body by placing ice or cold cloths on their wrists, neck, armpits, and groin area (where leg meets the hip)!
- Check the victim's **ABCs... Airway, Breathing, & Circulation**
- Stay with the victim until medical help arrives

Remember, **HEAT STROKE** is a medical emergency and can cause the victim to slip into a coma, so getting the victim's body temperature cooled down is more critical than getting fluids in their body!

What are <u>YOU</u> gonna do about...
INFECTION?

It is important to be very careful and protect yourself against the spread of disease or infection when caring for a wound that is bleeding. *(See TIPS ON FIRST AID AND SPREADING GERMS OR DISEASES at beginning of this section)*

INFECTION

Germs are the main cause of an infection and whenever you perform first aid on anyone (including yourself), there is always a chance of spreading germs or diseases. All injuries - from tiny cuts to massive wounds - <u>must</u> be cleaned immediately to reduce the chances of infection!

Things to watch for...
> **Sore or wound is red and swollen or has red streaks**
> **Sore or wound is warm or painful**
> **Wound may open and ooze clear or yellowish fluid**
> **Fever or muscle aches or stiffness in the neck**

What to do...
- ALWAYS wash your hands before <u>and</u> after caring for a wound... even if it is your own!
- Immediately wash minor wounds with soap and water or flush with hydrogen peroxide
- Cover wound with sterile bandage or gauze and change it daily
- Use an antibiotic cream or gel to help disinfect the wound and kill germs
- If infection gets worse, you may want to see a doctor

What are <u>YOU</u> gonna do about…POISONING?

Please make sure you have the local **Poison Control Center** phone number near a telephone since many poisonings can be cared for without the help of ambulance personnel. The people who staff Poison Control Centers (PCC) have access to information on most poisonous substances and can tell you what care to give to counteract the poison.

NATIONAL POISON CONTROL # 1-800-222-1222 (U.S. only)
Internet: http://www.1-800-222-1222.info

If outside U.S. write in your local Poison Control Centre phone # here:

_____

POISON - ABSORBED THROUGH THE SKIN

Things to watch for…
> **Reddened skin or burns**
> **Poison on skin or clothing**
> **Bites or puncture marks from insect or animal**
> *(see BITES & STINGS)*

What to do…
- Be aware and make sure it is safe…then ask what happened
- Move the victim to safety (away from the poison), if necessary
- Find the container (if any) or the name of the poison and call your local Poison Control Center or an ambulance
- Remove clothing that may have the poison on it and store them in a bag or someplace safe so people or animals won't touch them by accident!
- Flood skin with running water (hose or faucet) for 10 minutes or so
- Wash area gently with soap and water
- Monitor the victim's breathing and watch for any allergic reactions

POISON - INHALED BY BREATHING

Things to watch for…
> **Strong odors or fumes**
> **Find the source of the odor or fumes**
> **Difficulty in breathing or dizzy**

What to do...
- Be aware and make sure it is safe...then ask what happened
- Get the victim out to fresh air
- Avoid breathing the fumes and open windows and doors wide
- Call your local Poison Control Center or an ambulance
- If victim is not breathing, begin **Rescue Breathing**
  (see BREATHING PROBLEMS)

POISON - POISONOUS PLANTS (IVY, OAK, & SUMAC)

The most common poisonous plants found in Canada and the lower 48 states in the U.S. include:

Poison ivy - can grow as a shrub, a single-stemmed ground cover, or a trailing or climbing vine and is found throughout most of Canada and the U.S. The leaves usually come in leaflets of three to a stem and vary widely in color, size, shape and texture. *[see illustration 2-4 on page 62]*

Poison oak - can grow as a shrub, ground plant, or vine and is found throughout the West and Southwest (very common in Oregon and California). It also varies widely in shapes and colors but usually has the distinctive shape of an oak leaf. The leaves usually come in leaflets of three to a stem but can be in groups of five, seven or nine. It is best to learn what it looks like where you live. *[see illustration 2-5 on page 62]*

Poison sumac - is a tall shrub or small tree and mostly lives in swamps, bogs and other wet places. It has white berries and bright green, pointy leaves that grow 6 to 10 leaves per stem with one leaf on the tip and the rest on both sides of the stem. *[see illustration 2-6 on page 63]*

All 3 of these plants have a sap called **urushiol** (pronounced oo-roo-she-ol) which is a sticky, colorless oil that stains things black when exposed to air. The rash is caused by your reaction to this oil and can show up as quickly as a few hours or several days.

NOTE: The rash itself is <u>not</u> contagious but the OIL (urushiol) is what is transferred by hands, fingers, or clothing!! Make sure you wash your hands after touching the rash to avoid spreading the urushiol!

Things to watch for...
    Inflamed red rash
    Extremely itchy skin
    Blisters
    Swelling or fever

What to do...
- It is CRITICAL to wash the affected area thoroughly with soap and water and follow up with rubbing alcohol.
- Make sure you immediately remove and wash any clothing or shoes that got exposed to the poison
- If a rash or open sores develop, apply a paste of baking soda and water several times a day or use a calamine lotion on the area
- If condition gets worse or spreads onto large areas of the body or face, see a doctor

To relieve pain from poison ivy, oak, or sumac:

Jewelweed - If in the wilderness, a plant that grows near poison ivy called jewelweed (tiny, orange-yellow, cornucopia-shaped flowers with reddish or white spots) can be used directly on the rash or on the area that was brushed against the ivy. Crush the leaves and the juicy stems in your hands and apply to the area - even if there is no rash yet since it may help prevent a reaction! *[see illustration 2-7 on page 63]*

Baking soda - For a paste mix 3 parts baking soda with 1 part water or dissolve ½ to 1 cup in your bath.

Cider vinegar - Mix 1 part cider vinegar with 10 parts water and wash area or soak a cloth and apply that to the area.

Fresh mud or clay mudpack - Leave on until it dries and shower it off. (DO NOT use this method if <u>any</u> of the skin is broken or cracked to prevent infection!)

Illustration 2-4
Poison Ivy

Illustration 2-5
Poison Oak

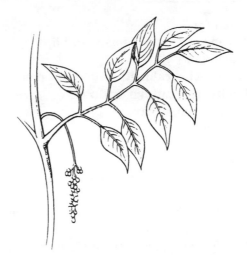

Illustration 2-6
Poison Sumac

Illustration 2-7
Jewelweed

POISON - SWALLOWED

Things to watch for...
> **Burns on the mouth, tongue and lips**
> **Stomach pains**
> **Open medicine cabinet; spilled or open containers**
> **Difficulty in breathing or dizzy**
> **Convulsions or seizures**
> **Passed out**

What to do...
- Find out exactly what, how much, and how long ago it was swallowed
- Call local Poison Control Center or an ambulance and have bottle/container handy
- NEVER give the victim anything to eat or drink unless told to do so by the Poison Control Center or a Medical professional!!
- If the victim pukes, lay them on their side to keep the airway open. Save a sample of the vomit IF the poison is unknown so the hospital can try to identify it.

It is a good idea to keep a few 1 ounce bottle of SYRUP OF IPECAC (pronounced ip'- î - kak) in your first aid kit and use only on the advice of a Medical professional or the Poison Control Center! (Syrup of Ipecac is sold by most pharmacies without a prescription.)

What are <u>YOU</u> gonna do about...
SHOCK?

Things to watch for...
> **Pale, cold, and clammy skin**
> **Rapid heartbeat but weak pulse**
> **Quick and shallow breathing**
> **Dizziness or confusion**
> **Bluish color on lips and fingertips or nails**
> **Sick to their stomach or puking**
> **Intense thirst**

What to do...
- Call for an ambulance
- Look for any injuries and monitor **ABCs... Airway, Breathing and Circulation**
- Position the victim using the following tips:

  <u>alert and awake</u> - place victim flat on their back with legs raised slightly

  <u>passed out or puking</u> - place victim on side to keep the airway open

- Loosen any tight or restrictive clothing
- Cover victim with a blanket or towel
- Talk calmly to the victim until help arrives (whether they are alert or not!)

What are <u>YOU</u> gonna do about…
A STROKE?

Strokes are one of the most common causes of death in North America. According to the National Stroke Association about 750,000 Americans suffer strokes each year and about one-fouth of those victims die. In Canada about 50,000 new strokes are reported annually and they are the 4th leading cause of death to Canadians according to the Heart and Stroke Foundation of Canada.

A stroke is caused by a lack of oxygen to the brain since the blood is not reaching it because…

> …a blood vessel bursts or leaks (sometimes called a bleeder) or
> …an artery is clogged by a large deposit of fatty tissue or a blood clot

NOTE: You only have 2 - 6 hours maximum to stop permanent brain damage from a stroke - so get to a hospital as quickly as possible (within 3 hours is best)! Most Emergency Rooms now have medicine to reduce the damaging long-term effects of a stroke - if the medication is given in time!

Things to watch for…
> **Slurring or mumbling**
> **Loss of balance or stumbling**
> **Different sized pupils (one pupil small and one pupil enlarged)**
> **Loss of muscle control on one side of the body**
> **Severe headache**
> **Blurred or double-vision**
> **Shock (pale, cold or clammy, drowsy, weak or rapid pulse, etc.)**

What to do…
- Call for an ambulance
- Get the victim to lie back with head raised (place pillows or blankets under head and shoulders so they're partially sitting up)
- Loosen any tight or restrictive clothing
- See if there are any other injuries
- If victim is drooling or having problems swallowing then place them on their side to keep the airway open
- Stay with victim until medical help arrives

www.fedhealth.net or call 1-888-999-4325

TIPS ON FIRST AID KITS

You should always be prepared and keep a First Aid Kit in your home <u>and</u> your car. If you like the outdoors (hiking, biking, etc.) you should carry a small kit in your fanny pack or backpack as a precaution. Always let your family know where the kits are in both the home and cars.

There are many different sizes of First Aid Kits on the market. Or you can make your own kits at home and we suggest you include the following products in a **<u>waterproof</u>** container or bag so you can be prepared for almost any type of emergency!

We realize there are a <u>lot</u> of items listed here and remember these are just suggestions, however, the more you are prepared... the better off you and your family will be in the event of a disaster!

*(See also **DISASTER SUPPLIES KIT** in **Section 3** which includes suggested items to include in mini kits for CAR and CLASSROOM or LOCKER or OFFICE)*

<u>Items to include in First Aid Kit</u>
Ace bandage(s)
Adhesive bandage strips in assorted sizes
Adhesive tape
Antibiotic ointment or gel
Antiseptic towelettes
Assorted sizes of safety pins
Box of Baking soda
Cleansing agent/soap
Cold pack
Contact lens solution and Eyewash solution
Cotton and Cotton swabs
Copy of *IT'S A DISASTER!* ...and what are YOU gonna do about it?
Disposable Face shield for Rescue Breathing
Disposable gloves
Flashlight and batteries - check regularly to make sure it works & batteries
  are good
Gauze pads
Hydrogen peroxide
Lip balm (one with SPF is best)

Moleskin (for blisters on feet)
Needle(s)
Plastic bags
Roller gauze
Scissors and tweezers
Small bottle of hand lotion
Snake bite kit with extractor
Sunscreen (choose one between SPF 15 and SPF 30)
Thermometer
Triangular bandages
Tube of petroleum jelly or other lubricant

Non-prescription drugs to include in First Aid Kit

Activated charcoal (use if advised by the Poison Control Center)
Anti-diarrhea medication
Antihistamine and decongestant (for allergic reactions or allergies and sinus problems)
Antacid (for upset stomach)
Aspirin, acetaminophen and ibuprofen
Laxative
Potassium Iodide *(see NUCLEAR POWER PLANT EMERGENCY section)*
Syrup of ipecac (used to induce vomiting only if advised by the Poison Control Center)

Tips on items that are inexpensive and widely available:

Activated charcoal - Absorbs poisons and drugs in the stomach and intestines and helps prevent toxins from being absorbed into the bloodstream by coating intestinal walls. (You should check with the Poison Control Center before taking since it doesn't work on all toxic substances.) It is available at natural foods stores and pharmacies in powder, liquid, and capsule forms. The capsules can also be broken open to use the powder for making a paste to apply on insect bites and stings.

Baking soda - aid for occasional heartburn or indigestion; use as substitute for toothpaste; sprinkle in bath water for sore muscles or bites & stings; or make a paste (3 parts baking soda to 1 part water) to use on bee stings & insect bites, poison ivy, canker sores, sunburn, and rashes (but is too strong for infants!)

Hydrogen peroxide - can help clean and disinfect wounds, treat canker sores, gingivitis, and minor earaches. (The reason it foams up on the skin is because of the oxygen at work.)

Meat tenderizer – use to make a paste for many kinds of bites and stings since it breaks down insect venom due to one main ingredient called "papain" (check ingredients for this word!)

Syrup of ipecac (pronounced ip'- î - kak) - use only when advised by the Poison Control Center to cause puking and is available at most pharmacies or drug stores in 1 oz bottles

Vinegar - Helps relieve jellyfish stings, sunburn, and swimmer's ear

Section 3

Disaster Preparedness

FAMILY DISASTER PLAN

Disasters happen anytime and anywhere. And when disaster strikes, you may not have much time to respond. Would your family be prepared to cope with the emergency until help arrives?

FIRST - DEVELOP A FAMILY DISASTER PLAN

See **Section 1 - Family Information & Personal Checklists** to help develop an **Emergency Plan** using the checklists similar to ones developed by the Red Cross and FEMA… after reading through this Manual!

SECOND - DEVELOP A DISASTER SUPPLIES KIT

Your family will cope best by preparing for disaster BEFORE it strikes. One way to prepare is by assembling a **DISASTER SUPPLIES KIT**.

Once disaster threatens or hits, you may not have time to shop or search for supplies. BUT… if you have gathered supplies in advance, your family can handle an evacuation or shelter living easier and it's all together in one place… all you gotta do is **GRAB & GO**!

Place these supplies you'd most likely need (water, food, first aid & emergency items, etc.) in a container that is easy-to-carry and that will fit in your vehicle. For example, a large trash can or storage container with a lid that snaps shut tightly (some even come with wheels), a waterproof backpack, or a large duffel bag (waterproof, if possible) would be useful.

We are also including suggestions for a **CAR KIT** and a **CLASSROOM or LOCKER or OFFICE KIT** since these are usually the most common places you would be if and when a disaster strikes!

DISASTER SUPPLIES KIT

There are six basic categories of supplies you should stock in your home: water, food, first aid supplies, tools and emergency supplies, clothing and bedding, and special items. (Also shown below are suggestions for a **CAR KIT** and a **CLASSROOM or LOCKER or OFFICE KIT**.)

Supplies should <u>ALL</u> be checked every 6 months to make sure they are still good and working! We suggest you mark dates on your calendar and have the entire family help check all the items together. Again, it will be good quality time with the family and it will give you all a chance to update any phone numbers or information that has changed.

WATER

A normally active person needs to drink at least 2 quarts (2 litres) of water each day and possibly as much as a gallon (4 litres) a day. *(See **TIPS ON WATER PURIFICATION** in next section.)*

[ ] Store one gallon of water per person per day (two quarts/litres for drinking and two quarts/litres for food preparation and sanitation).

[ ] Keep at <u>least</u> a three-day supply of water for each person in your household. Rotate new bottles every 6 months.

[ ] Store an extra bottle if you have a pet so you don't reduce your amount.

FOOD

Select foods that require no refrigeration, preparation or cooking and little or no water. If you must heat food, pack a can of sterno. Select food items that are compact and lightweight. Rotate out food in Kit every 6 months.

[ ] Ready-to-eat canned meats, fish, fruits, and vegetables (and include a <u>manual can opener</u>!!)

[ ] Canned juices, milk, soup (if powdered or cubes, store extra water!)

[ ] Staples - sugar, salt, pepper

[ ] High energy foods - peanut butter, jelly, crackers, granola bars, trail mix, nuts, jerky, dried fruits, Emergency Food bars, etc.

[ ] Vitamins & herbs (e.g. a good multiple, extra C & E, Echinacea, St. John's Wort, etc.)

[ ] Foods for infants, elderly persons or persons on special diets

[ ] Foods for your pet (if you have one)

[ ] Comfort/stress foods - cookies, hard candy, sweetened cereal, suckers, instant coffee, tea bags

[ ] Some companies offer survival and long-term storage foods that are freeze dried and sold in several months, 1 year, and 2 year supplies

FIRST AID KITS

There are many different sizes of First Aid Kits on the market. Or you can make your own kits at home and we suggest you have these products in a **waterproof** container or bag and have one in the Home and in every Car (see below for suggestions on CAR KIT)!

See **TIPS ON FIRST AID KITS** at end of **Section 2**.

TOOLS AND SUPPLIES

[ ] Paper cups, plates and plastic utensils (or Mess Kits) and paper towels

[ ] A copy of this Manual (*IT'S A DISASTER!* ...and what are YOU gonna do about it?)

[ ] Battery operated radio and extra batteries (remember to check batteries every 6 months)

[ ] Flashlight and extra batteries & extra bulbs (check every 6 months)

[ ] Cash or traveler's check and some change

[ ] Manual can opener and a utility knife

[ ] Fire extinguisher: small canister, ABC type

[ ] Tube tent or plastic sheeting (for shelter or lean-to)

[ ] Pliers

[ ] Tape (plastic & duct)

[ ] Compass

[ ] Matches in a waterproof container and candles

[ ] Aluminum foil

[ ] Sterno or small camp stove and mini propane bottle

[ ] Signal flare

[ ] Paper, pencil (store in baggies to keep dry)

[ ] Needles, thread

[ ] Medicine dropper (various uses – use to measure drops of bleach to purify water, etc.)

[ ] Wrench (to turn off household gas and water)

[ ] Whistle (can be used to call for help in an emergency)

[ ] Map of the area (to help locate shelters)

[ ] Work gloves

SANITATION

Make sure all these items are in a waterproof containers or plastic bags.

[ ] Toilet paper, baby wipes

[ ] Soap, liquid detergent, or waterless hand sanitizer

[ ] Feminine supplies (tampons, pads, etc.)

[ ] Personal hygiene items (toothbrushes, toothpaste or baking soda, brush, comb, etc.)

[ ] Plastic garbage bags, ties (for personal sanitation uses)

[ ] Plastic bucket with tight lid (for human waste use)

[ ] Disinfectant *(See next section on TIPS ON SANITATION OF HUMAN WASTE)*

[ ] Household chlorine bleach (regular scent)

CLOTHING AND BEDDING

[ ] Include at least one complete change of clothing and footwear per person.

[ ] Sturdy shoes or work boots and extra socks

[ ] Rain gear or poncho (small emergency ones are cheap and about the size of a wallet or use plastic garbage bags)

[ ] Blankets or sleeping bags (small emergency ones are cheap and about the size of a wallet or pack extra garbage bags)

[ ] Hat and gloves and Thermal underwear

[ ] Safety glasses and/or Sunglasses

[ ] Small stuffed animal, toy or book for each child

SPECIAL ITEMS

[ ] Entertainment - games, books and playing cards

[ ] RED and GREEN construction paper or RED and GREEN crayons or markers

[ ] Important Family Documents (keep in waterproof, portable safe container and update when necessary!)

> — Extra set of car keys and cash, traveler's checks and a credit card
> — Will, insurance policies, contracts, deeds, stocks and bonds
> — Passports, social security cards, immunization records
> — Bank account numbers
> — Credit card numbers and companies
> — Inventory of valuable household goods, important phone numbers
> — Family records (birth, marriage, death certificates)
> — Recent pictures of all family members and pets for identification needs

Remember family members with special needs such as Infants, Elderly and Disabled persons:

For Infants

[ ] Formula

[ ] Diapers

[ ] Bottles

[ ] Powdered milk

[ ] Medications

[ ] Small soft toys

For Elderly and Disabled (Children & Adults)

[ ] Prescription drugs

[ ] Special medicines for Heart, high blood pressure and/or Diabetes (insulin)

[ ] Extra eye glasses or contact lenses and supplies

[ ] Denture needs

[ ] Adult bladder control garments and pads

[ ] Extra hearing aid batteries

[ ] A list of the style and serial numbers of medical devices such as pacemakers

[ ] Extra wheelchair batteries, oxygen, catheters or other special equipment

[ ] Store backup equipment, such as a manual wheelchair, cane or walker at a neighbor's home or at another location

CAR KIT

Keep most or all of these items in a waterproof pack so everything is together and easy to grab. Make one for each vehicle too!

[ ] Battery-powered radio, flashlight, extra batteries and extra bulbs

[ ] First Aid Kit

[ ] Local maps

[ ] Blanket (small emergency ones are cheap and about the size of a wallet)

[ ] Extra clothes (jeans and sweater), sturdy shoes and socks

[ ] Shovel (small collapsible ones are available)

[ ] Work gloves

[ ] Tools - Tire repair kit, booster cables, flares, screw driver, pliers, knife, wire

[ ] Short rubber hose (for siphoning)

[ ] Bottled water and non-perishable foods (store food in empty coffee cans to keep it from getting squashed)

[ ] Plastic bags that seal

[ ] Small fire extinguisher (5 lb., ABC type)

[ ] A copy of this Manual (*IT'S A DISASTER!* ...and what are you gonna do about it?)

CLASSROOM OR LOCKER OR OFFICE KIT

Keep items in a small pack, drawstring bag or duffle so everything is together and easy to grab!

[ ] Small first aid kit

[ ] Battery-operated radio and extra batteries

[ ] Mini or regular flashlight and extra bulbs and batteries

[ ] A few plastic trash bags

[ ] Work gloves to protect your hands (especially due to broken glass)

[ ] Sweatshirt or sweater

[ ] Emergency blanket (small, cheap, & light and about the size of a wallet)

[ ] Non-perishable foods like crackers, cookies, trail mix, granola bars, etc. (Ask children to help with choosing the food and make sure they understand this is for Emergencies!)

[ ] Small (plastic) bottled water or juice… or as much as you can fit in your kit!

[ ] Small stuffed animal, book, or toy for children

[ ] Small packet of tissues

[ ] Small packet of moist towelettes or mini bottle of hand sanitizer (waterless kind)

[ ] A copy of this Manual (*IT'S A DISASTER!* …and what are YOU gonna do about it?)

SUGGESTIONS & REMINDERS ABOUT KITS

- Store your **DISASTER SUPPLIES KIT** in a convenient place known to ALL family members. Keep a smaller version (**CAR KIT**) in the trunk/back of every vehicle.

- Keep items in airtight plastic bags.

- Replace your stored food and water supply every 6 months! It's best to test or replace the batteries at this time too. Make a game of it by keeping track on a calendar or on a poster drawn by the children so they can help! Also, the FAMILY should meet every 6 months anyway to go over the **Emergency Plan** and update any data (phone numbers, address changes, etc.)

- Ask your physician or pharmacist about storing prescription medicines.

TIPS ON USING HOUSEHOLD FOODS

Cooking in a Disaster Situation

When disaster strikes, you may not have electricity or gas for cooking. For emergency cooking you can use a charcoal grill, hibachi or propane camping unit or stove - but only do this <u>OUTDOORS</u>! **Never** use charcoal in an enclosed environment since it causes deadly fumes!

You can also heat food with candle warmers or a can of sterno.

Canned food can be heated in the can, but remember to remove the paper label and open the can first! And be careful and don't burn your hand since it may be hot!

If the electricity goes off, use your food wisely...

First - use perishable food and foods from the refrigerator... and limit opening the frig (don't stand and stare in it like we all normally do!)

Second - Use foods from the freezer and, if possible, have a list of items in the freezer on the outside to cut down on opening the door! Foods in a well-filled, well-insulated freezer will not go bad until several days after the power goes off. Usually there will be ice crystals in the center of the food (which means it's okay to eat) for at least 3 days after a power failure.

Third - Use non-perishable foods and staples in your pantry and cupboards.

TIP FOR YOUR FREEZER: Before a disaster strikes, line your freezer wall with jugs of frozen water. Save empty fruit juice bottles or plastic milk jugs and disinfect them with a small amount of regular scent household bleach. (Make sure to swish the bleach around real good to clean the entire jug and handle!)

Let it air dry for an hour or so, then fill with clean water. Place bottle or jug in freezer and it will help keep food cold longer if you lose power and you'll have extra water once it melts! This also helps keep the freezer as full as possible which makes it more energy efficient!

TIPS ON WATER PURIFICATION

Water is critical for survival. We can go days, even weeks, without food but we <u>must</u> have water to live.   For example, the average man (154 pounds) can lose about 3 quarts/litres of water per day and the average woman (140 pounds) can lose over 2 litres - and this increases depending on your weight and size, on the time of the year, and the altitude!

Your body can lose precious water by sweating and breathing - whether you feel it or not – and, of course, by peeing. In fact, the color of your pee will tell you if you are getting dehydrated! When you drink enough water, your pee will be a light-colored or bright yellow, but when you are dehydrated it will be dark-colored and you'll pee in small amounts.

The average person should drink between 2 and 2 ½ quarts/litres of water per day.   We suggest you plan on storing about one gallon (4 litres) per day per person to cover for drinking, cooking and personal hygiene - and don't forget about your pets!

Did you know…
… according to U.N. figures, a child dies every 8 seconds from water-related disease?
… and unsafe water causes 3.3 <u>billion</u> cases of illness and 5 <u>million</u> deaths worldwide each year?

Use any of the following methods to purify drinking water:

<u>Boiling</u> — Boil vigorously for 7-10 minutes..

<u>Bleach</u> — Add 10-20 drops of household bleach per gallon (about 4 litres) of water, mix well and let stand for 30 minutes. A slight smell or taste of chlorine indicates water is good to drink. (NOTE: Do <u>NOT</u> use scented bleaches, colorsafe bleaches or bleaches with added cleaners!)

<u>Tablets</u> — Use commercial purification tablets and follow instructions.

<u>Stabilized oxygen</u> — Use 10 drops of stabilized oxygen per gallon/4 litres of water to help prevent the growth of certain bacteria. (To store water for long periods of time use 20 drops per gallon/4 litres.)

Also, learn how to remove the water in the hot water heater and in other water supplies in your home or office. A few examples of other water supplies include ice cubes and your toilet tank (<u>not</u> the bowl and <u>don't</u> use it if chemicals are in the tank!)

TIPS ON SANITATION OF HUMAN WASTE

In disaster situations, plumbing may not be usable, due to broken sewer lines, broken water lines, flooding, or freezing of the system. To avoid the spread of disease, it is critical that human waste be handled in a sanitary manner!

IF TOILET OKAY BUT LINES ARE NOT...
If the water or sewer lines are damaged but the toilet is still intact, you should line the toilet bowl with a plastic bag to collect waste... but DO NOT flush the toilet!!! After use, a small amount of disinfectant should be added to the bag, and the bag sealed and placed in a tightly covered container, away from people.

IF TOILET IS UNUSABLE...
If toilet itself is unusable, a plastic bag in a bucket may be substituted. After use, a small amount of disinfectant should be added to the bag and the bucket should be covered tightly with a lid.

Disinfectants - easy and effective for home use in Sanitation of Human Waste. Choose one to store with your Disaster Supplies Kit:

Chlorine Bleach - If water is available, a solution of 1 part liquid household chlorine bleach to 10 parts water is best. DO NOT use dry bleach, which is caustic (can burn you, corrode, or dissolve) and is not safe for this kind of use.

Calcium hypochlorite - (e.g. HTH, etc.) is available in swimming pool supply stores and several large discount stores. It can be used in solution by mixing, then storing. Follow directions on the package.

Portable toilet chemicals - These come in both liquid and dry formulas and are available at recreational vehicle (RV) supply stores. Use according to package directions. These chemicals are designed especially for toilets that are not connected to sewer lines.

Powdered, chlorinated lime - Available at some building supply stores. It can be used dry and be sure to get chlorinated lime - *not* quick lime!

There are also several types of camping toilets and portable toilets that can be purchased in camping stores and on the Internet that range from fairly low dollars to hundreds of dollars.

WHAT TO DO **<u>BEFORE</u>** A DISASTER STRIKES (MITIGATION TIPS)...

There are many things you can do to protect yourself, your home and your property BEFORE any type of natural hazard or disaster strikes!

Please realize that natural disasters have some common elements that overlap (like wind and floods) and we are only summarizing some key topics here to help get you started. There are many mitigation tips and programs available from government agencies, public and private businesses, nonprofits and NGOs listed here and in Section 4 of this book that can help you and your family learn more.

WHAT IS MITIGATION?

Mitigation simply means an effort to lessen the impact disasters have on people, property, communities and the economy. It is also about reducing the risks and involves planning, commitment, preparation and communication between local and federal government officials, businesses and the general public.

Some examples of mitigation include installing hurricane straps to secure a structure's roof to its walls and foundation, building outside of flood plains, securing shelves and other loose objects inside and around the home, developing and enforcing effective building codes and standards, using fire-retardant materials, and the list goes on and on.

Soon we will explain what to do BEFORE, DURING and AFTER specific types of natural and man-made disasters. But first there are some things you should do in advance that take time and planning - otherwise known as prevention or mitigation tips! First we'll cover some tips on the two most common disasters (winds and floods) then we'll list others alphabetically.

MITIGATION TIPS TO HELP PREVENT DAMAGE AND LOSS:

<u>WIND MITIGATION</u>

Wind damage is the most common disaster-related expense and usually accounts for about 70% or more of the insured losses reported worldwide. Many natural disasters like hurricanes, tornadoes, thunderstorms, microbursts, and winter storms include damaging winds. And certain parts of the world experience high winds on a normal basis due to wind patterns.

Realize when extreme winds strike they are not constant - they rapidly increase and decrease. A home in the path of wind causes the wind to change direction. This change in wind direction increases pressure on parts of the house creating stress which causes the connections between building components to fail. For example, the roof or siding can be pulled off or the windows can be pushed in.

Strengthen weak spots on home

Experts believe there are four areas of your home that should be checked for weakness -- the roof, windows, doors and garage doors. Homeowners can take some steps to secure and strengthen these areas but some things should be done by an experienced builder or contractor.

ROOF:
- Truss bracing or gable end bracing (supports placed strategically to strengthen the roof)
- Anchors, clips and straps can be installed (may want to call a professional since sometimes difficult to install)

WINDOWS and DOORS:
- Storm shutters (available for windows, French doors, sliding glass doors, and skylights) or keep plywood on hand
- Reinforced bolt kits for doors

GARAGE DOORS:
- Certain parts of the country have building codes requiring garage doors to withstand high winds (check with local building officials)
- Some garage doors can be strenthened with retrofit kits (involves installing horizontal bracing onto each panel)

Secure mobile homes

Make sure your trailer or mobile home is securely anchored. Consult the manufacturer for information on secure tiedown systems.

Secure or tie down loose stuff

Extreme winds can also cause damage from flying debris that can act like missiles and ram through walls, windows or the roof if the wind speeds are high enough. You should consider securing large or heavy equipment inside and out to reduce some of the flying debris like patio furniture, barbeque grills, water heaters, garbage cans, bookcases and shelving, etc.

Consider building a shelter or "safe room"

Shelters or "safe rooms" are designed to provide protection from the high winds expected during hurricanes, tornadoes and from flying debris.

FEMA provides an excellent free booklet called "Taking Shelter From the Storm: Building a Safe Room Inside Your House" developed in association with the Wind Engineering Research Center at Texas Tech University. You can learn more by visiting http://www.fema.gov/mit/saferoom/

FLOOD MITIGATION

Flood damage is normally the second most common disaster-related expense of insured losses reported worldwide. Many natural disasters like hurricanes, tornadoes, rain, thunderstorms, and melting snow and ice cause flooding. And there are certain parts of North America that are known as "flood plains" and are at high risk of floods.

But I have insurance...

Insurance companies will cover some claims due to water damage like a broken water main or a washing machine that goes berserk. However, standard home insurance policies DO NOT generally cover flood damage caused by natural events or disasters!

The United States offers a **National Flood Insurance Program** available in most communities and there is a waiting period for coverage. Talk to your local insurance agent or contact NFIP directly at 1-800-427-4771.

Currently Canadians do not have a national flood program, however, there are certain parts of Canada that offer limited flood-damage coverage but it must be purchased year-round and the rates are relatively high. The Insurance Bureau of Canada suggests you consult your insurance representative with questions regarding coverage.

Move valuables to higher ground

If your home or business is prone to flooding, you should move valuables and appliances out of the basement or ground level floors.

Elevate breakers, fuse box and meters

Consider phoning a professional to elevate the main breaker or fuse box and utility meters above the anticipated flood level so flood waters won't damage your utilities.

The next few pages cover some key mitigation tips on several types of disasters (sorted alphabetically). After this mitigation section we cover many natural and man-made disasters in more detail.

Remember... the more you prepare BEFORE disaster strikes, the better off you and your loved ones will be financially, emotionally and physically!

EARTHQUAKE MITIGATION

A lot of the ongoing research by scientists, engineers and emergency preparedness officials has resulted in improvements to building codes around the world. Proven design and construction techniques are available that help limit damage and injuries.

There are also some mitigation measures consumers can take to reduce risk if you live in an earthquake-prone area:

Consider retrofitting your home

There are options to retrofit or reinforce your home's foundation and frame available from reputable contractors who follow strict building codes.

Other earthquake-safety measures include installing flexible gas lines and automatic gas shutoff valves. Changes to gas lines and plumbing in your house must be done by a licensed contractor, who will ensure that the work is done correctly and according to all applicable codes. This is important for your safety.

Secure loose stuff

- Use nylon straps or L-braces to secure cupboards, bookcases and other tall furniture to the wall.
- Secure heavy appliances like water heaters, refrigerators, etc. using bands of perforated steel (also known as "plumber's tape").
- Use buckles or safety straps to secure computers, televisions, stereos and other equipment to tabletops.
- Use earthquake or florist putty to tack down glassware, heirlooms and figurines

FIRE MITIGATION

Home fire protection is very important and covered on pages 106-107. Also see Wildfire Mitigation to learn additional ways to protect your home.

LIGHTNING MITIGATION

Here are some safety tips to prepare your home for lightning.

Install a Lightning Protection System

A lightning protection system does not prevent lightning from striking but does create a direct path for lightning to follow. Basically, a lightning protection system consists of air terminals (lightning rods) and associated fittings connected by heavy cables to grounding equipment. This provides a path for lightning current to travel safely to the ground.

Install surge protectors on or in home

Surge protection devices (SPDs) can be installed in the electrical panel to protect your entire home from electrical surges. Sometimes it may be necessary to install small individual SPDs in addition to the home unit for computers and television sets due to different ratings and voltage levels.

If a home unit is too expensive, consider getting individual surge protection devices that plug into the wall for the refrigerator, microwave and garage door openers. Appliances that use two services (cable wire and electrical cord) may require combination SPDs for computers, TVs, and VCRs.

WILDFIRE MITIGATION

As our population continues to grow, more and more people are building homes in places that were once pristine wilderness areas. Homeowners who build in remote and wooded areas must take responsibility for the way their buildings are constructed and the way they landscape around them.

Use Fire Resistant Building Materials

The roof and exterior structure of your home and other buildings should be constructed of non-combustible or fire-resistant materials. If wood siding, cedar shakes or any other highly combustible materials are used, they should be treated with fire retardant chemicals.

Landscape wisely

Plant fire-resistant shrubs and trees to minimize the spread of fire and space your landscaping so that fire is not carried to your home or other surrounding vegetation. Remove vines from the walls of your home.

Create a "safety zone" around the house
- Mow grass regularly.
- Stack firewood at least 100 ft (30 m) away and uphill from home.

- Keep your roof and gutters free of pine needles, leaves, and branches and clear away flammable vegetation at least 30 to 100 feet (9 to 30 m) from around your structures.
- Thin a 15-foot (4.5 m) space between tree crowns and remove limbs within 10-15 feet (3-4.5 m) of the ground.
- Remove dead branches that extend over the roof.
- Prune tree branches and shrubs within 10 feet (3 m) of a stovepipe or chimney outlet.
- Remove leaves and rubbish from under structures
- Ask the power company to clear branches from power lines.
- Keep combustibles away from structures and clear a 10-foot (3 m) area around propane tanks, barbeques, boats, etc.

Protect your home
- Install smoke detectors, test them each month and change batteries once a year.
- Consider installing protective shutters or heavy fire-resistant drapes
- Inspect chimneys at least twice a year and clean every year
- Cover chimney and stovepipe flue openings with 1/2 inch (1 cm) or smaller non-flammable mesh screen
- Use this same mesh screen beneath porches, decks, floor areas and the home itself. Also screen openings to attic and roof.
- Soak ashes and charcoal briquettes in water for two days in a metal bucket
- Keep a garden hose connected to an outlet
- Have fire tools handy (ladder, shovel, rake, saw, ax, bucket, etc.)
- Address should be visible on all structures and seen from the road

WINTER STORM & EXTREME COLD MITIGATION
Severe winter weather causes deterioration and damage to homes every year. There are many things you can do to prepare for the bitter cold, ice and snow in advance to save you money and headaches in the long run. Some of these tips should be used by apartment dwellers too!

"Winterize" your home
- Insulate walls and attic
- Caulk and weather-strip doors and windows to keep cold out
- Install storm windows or cover windows with plastic film from the inside to keep warmth in
- Detach garden hoses and shut-off water supply to those faucets
- Install faucet covers or wrap them tightly with towels and duct tape

- Show family members the location of your main water valve and mark it so you can find it quickly
- Drain sprinkler water lines or well lines before the first freeze
- Keep the inside temperature of your home at 68 degrees Fahrenheit (20 degrees Celsius) or higher, even if you are leaving
- Wrap pipes near exterior walls with heating tape or towels
- Change furnace filters regularly and have it serviced periodically
- Make sure you have good lighting from the street and driveway to help others see snow and ice patches and try to keep paths clear
- Remove dead tree branches since they break easily
- Cover fireplace and stovepipe openings with fire-resistant screens
- Check shingles to make sure they are in good shape

Preventing "ice dams"

A lot of water leakage and damage around outside walls and ceilings are actually due to "ice dams". Ice dams are lumps of ice that form on gutters or downspouts and eavestroughs and prevent melting snow from running down. An attic with no insulation (like a detached garage) or a well-sealed and insulated attic will generally not have ice dams. But if the roof has many peaks and valleys, is poorly insulated, or has a large roof overhang, ice dams usually happen.

Some tips to prevent ice dams:
- Keep gutters and downspouts clear of leaves, twigs and debris
- Find areas of heat loss in attic and insulate it properly
- Wrap or insulate heating duct work to reduce heat loss
- Remove snow buildup on roof and gutters using a snow rake or soft broom
- Consider installing roof heat tapes (electric cables) that clip onto the edge of your shingles to melt channels in the ice (but realize the cables use a lot of energy and may not be too attractive but may help on older homes with complicated roofs)

Preventing frozen pipes

- Keep cabinet doors open under sinks so heat can circulate
- Run a slow trickle of lukewarm water and check water flow before going to bed and when you get up. (The first sign of freezing is reduced water flow so keep an eye on it!)
- Heat your basement or at least insulate it well!
- Close windows and keep drafts away from pipes since air flow can cause pipes to freeze more often.

MITIGATION TIPS SUMMARY...

Take responsibility...
Basically, no matter where you live, you should take personal responsibility and prepare yourself, your family and your property BEFORE disasters or natural hazards strike.

...and learn more!
After reviewing the remainder of this book, please contact your local emergency officials or your local building department to learn about all the risks in your area and what to expect if disaster strikes.

Remember, the best thing you can do to deal with any type of disaster is...

BE AWARE... **BE PREPARED**... and... **HAVE A PLAN**!

If you do these 3 things, the life and property you save could be your own... because what you <u>don't</u> know <u>CAN</u> hurt you!

MITIGATION STRATEGIES FOR BUSINESSES & CONSUMERS

Both the U.S. and Canada have national programs designed to help the public, businesses and communities prepare for the unexpected.

In the U.S., the Pre-Disaster Mitigation Program (PDM) builds on the experience gained from previous community-based disaster mitigation grants, the Hazard Mitigation Grant Program, and other initiatives like Project Impact. And FEMA recently united the Federal Insurance Administration and the Mitigation Directorate to create the Federal Insurance and Mitigation Administration (FIMA). FIMA combines organizational activities to promote Protection, Prevention, and Partnerships at the Federal, State, local and individual levels to lessen the impact of disasters upon families, homes, communities and economy. To learn more please visit FIMA online at http://www.fema.gov/fima/

In Canada, SAFE GUARD is a national information program aimed at increasing awareness of emergency preparedness. Originally an Emergency Preparedness Canada initiative, SAFE GUARD has now developed into a partnership of organizations with a defined role or interest in ensuring and promoting the safety and security of Canadians through all levels of government, NGOs, businesses and associations. *(Please see **APPENDIX B** for more information about SAFE GUARD.)*

WHAT TO EXPECT WHEN A DISASTER STRIKES...

Local government and disaster-relief organizations will try to help you but there are <u>many</u> times they cannot reach you immediately after a disaster.

You should be ready to be self-sufficient for at *least* three days... possibly longer depending on the type of disaster!

This may mean providing for your own shelter, food, water and sanitation.

If you have planned ahead, it will be easier to recover from a disaster as long as you have your **Disaster Supplies Kit** and an **Emergency Plan** for you and your family. This can help reduce some of the fear, anxiety and losses that surround a disaster.

By planning ahead, you will know where to go, be ready to evacuate if necessary, and be a little more comfortable in a shelter by having some of your own personal items with you in your **Disaster Supplies Kit**.

Now we are going to explain what to do **BEFORE**, **DURING** and **AFTER** specific types of natural and man-made disasters. There are also sections on **RECOVERING FROM A DISASTER** (includes many "AFTER" tips that apply to most every type of disaster) and on **SHELTER LIVING**.

As we mentioned in the Introduction, a majority of this information was compiled from various publications provided by the Red Cross, FEMA, Canada's OCIPEP and others to help assist you in preparing for various types disasters.

We realize you may not experience every type of disaster in your part of the world but if you ever travel away from home you could potentially be placed in a disaster situation so please educate yourself and your family.

What are <u>YOU</u> gonna do about...
AVALANCHES, LANDSLIDES & MUDFLOWS?

Avalanches - masses of loosened snow or ice that tumble down the side of a mountain, often growing as it descends picking up mud, rocks, trees and debris triggered by various means including wind, rapid warming, snow conditions and humans.

Landslides - masses of rock, earth or debris that move down a slope and can be caused by earthquakes, volcanic eruptions, and by humans who develop on land that is unstable.

Mudflows - rivers of rock, earth, and other debris soaked with water mostly caused by melting snow or heavy rains and create a "slurry". A "slurry" can travel several miles from its source and grows in size as it picks up trees, cars, and other things along the way just like an avalanche!

Please realize data on avalanches fill up entire books and we are only touching on some basic information here with some references to obtain more information, then we'll briefly cover landslides and mudflows.

Avalanche Basics

Snow avalanches are a natural process and happen about a million times per year worldwide. Contrary to what is shown in the movies, avalanches are <u>not</u> triggered by loud noises like a shout or a sonic boom -- it's just not enough force. An avalanche is actually formed by a combination of several things -- a steep slope (the terrain), the snowpack, a weak layer in the snowpack, and a natural or artificial "trigger".

Nearly all avalanches that involve people are triggered by the victim or a member of their party. Each year avalanches claim between 100-200 lives around the world and thousands of people are partly buried or injured in them.

Millions of skiers, hikers, climbers, snowshoers, snowboarders, and snowmobilers venture out every year to enjoy winter sports forcing activities, roads, buildings and towns into avalanche-prone areas. Compound that with recreationists who cross into the backcountry with little or no basic avalanche training... and you've got a recipe for potential disaster!

Types of avalanches

<u>Slab</u> - the most dangerous type of avalanche since it causes most fatalities. Experts compare slab avalanches to a dinner plate sliding off the table - a heavier plate of snow slides on top of weaker snow down a slope. An average-sized dry slab avalanche travels about 80 mph (128 km/h) and it's nearly impossible to outrun it or get out of the way!

Most avalanche deaths are caused by slab even though there are many obvious signs that indicate danger -- so educate yourself before venturing out into the backcountry!

<u>Powder or loose snow</u> - fresh fallen, light, dry snow (similar to fine sugar) rolls downhill with speeds of 110-180 mph (180-290 km/h) and swirls of powder climbing several thousand feet into the air. This is the most common type of avalanche and the danger is usually not the weight or volume but rather victims being pushed over a cliff or into a tree.

Some other types of avalanches include **ice falls**, **wet** and **point release**. You can find more information on the Internet at the North American Avalanche Centers' web site <u>www.avalanche.org</u> or visit your local library.

<u>Typical Avalanche Victims</u>

Nearly everyone caught in an avalanche is either skiing, snowboarding, riding a snowmobile, snowshoeing, hiking or climbing in the backcountry and they, or someone in their party, almost always trigger the avalanche that kills them. According to the American Avalanche Association the majority of victims are white, educated men between the ages of 18-35 who are very skilled at their sport.

One key is for the public to take personal responsibility and learn more about avalanche risks and safety procedures. The AAA has seen an increase in attendance now that avalanche educators are re-designing their courses to accommodate snowmobilers, snowboarders and other groups.

People should be prepared and learn how to recognize, assess and avoid avalanche danger by taking an avalanche-related course <u>before</u> entering the backcountry.

<u>The "Avalanche Triangle"</u>

The following information was excerpted from the **USDA Forest Service National Avalanche Center's** web site under "Avalanche Basics":

Avalanches are formed by a combination of 3 ingredients (sometimes called the "avalanche triangle")...

Terrain - the slope must be steeper than 25 degrees and most often occur on slopes between 35 and 45 degrees. Most slab avalanches occur on slopes with starting zone angels between about 30 and 45 degrees.

Snowpack - the snowpack accumulates layer by layer with each weather event and both strong and weak layers exist. Strong layers contain small round snow grains that are packed closely together and well bonded (or cohesive). Weak layers are less dense and appear loose or "sugary". When a strong dense layer is over a weak less dense layer it's like a brick on top of potato chips -- the chips can't hold up the weight of the brick so an avalanche occurs. Backcountry recreationists must learn the relationship of these layers because weak layers prevent strong layers from bonding with one another thus causing unstable conditions.

A snowpack is balanced between stress and strength -- add additional stress (like more snow or a human) and an avalanche could be triggered.

Weather - precipitation, wind and temperature can alter the stability of the snowpack by changing the balance between stress and strength. The type of precipitation and at what rate it falls are equally as important as the amount. If a lot of snow falls in a short amount of time, the snowpack has less time to adjust to the additional stress. Wind can blow large amounts of snow around shifting the stress on the snowpack. And rapid warming temperatures can cause snowpacks to become very wet and unstable.

BEFORE AN AVALANCHE:

1. Learn about local risks by contacting the local emergency management office *(see Section 4 for State & Provincial listing),* especially if you are visiting or moving to an "avalanche-prone" area.

2. Take an avalanche safety training course from a professional trainer or educator! Avalanche educators offer a variety of courses and levels ranging from recreational novices to backcountry experts. Visit www.avalanche.org and click on "Education".

3. Learn the Avalanche Danger Scales and corresponding colors used where you live or plan on visiting.

4. Carry avalanche rescue equipment or gear like portable shovels, collapsible probes or ski-pole probes, high frequency avalanche beacons

(transceivers), etc. and learn how to use it! Remember... just having avalanche equipment will NOT keep you out of an avalanche!!

5. Check weather forecasts and avalanche advisories before going out.

6. Switch beacon on prior to entering the backcountry! Check the battery strength and verify the "transmit" and "receive" functionality with everyone in your group to ensure beacons are picking up both signals.

7. Before crossing a snow covered slope in avalanche terrain, fasten your clothing securely to keep snow out and remove your ski pole straps.

DURING AN AVALANCHE:

Bail - try out get out of the way if possible! (For example, if a skier or boarder - ski out diagonally... if on a snowmobile - drive downhill, etc.)

If YOU are caught in the avalanche...

Scream and drop it - Yell and drop your ski poles (or anything in your hands) so they don't drag you down

Start swimming - Use "swimming" motions, thrusting upward to try to stay near the surface of the snow

Prepare to make an air pocket - try to keep your arms and hands moving so the instant the avalanche stops you can make an air pocket in front of your face by punching in the snow around you before it sets

If you see SOMEONE ELSE caught in the avalanche...

Watch - watch them closely as they are carried downhill, paying particular attention to the last point you saw them

AFTER AN AVALANCHE:

If YOU are caught in the avalanche...

Make an air pocket ASAP! - the INSTANT the avalanche stops try to maintain an air pocket in front of your face by using your hands and arms to punch in the snow and make a pocket of air. (You only have 1-3 seconds before the snow sets -- and most deaths are due to suffocation!)

Stick it out - If you are lucky enough to be near the surface, try to stick out an arm or a leg so that rescuers can find you

Don't panic - keep your breathing steady to help preserve your air space and help your body conserve energy

<u>Listen for rescuers</u> - since snow is such a good insulator the rescuers probably won't even hear you until they are practically on top of you so don't start yelling until you hear them. (This will conserve your precious air!)

If you see SOMEONE ELSE caught in the avalanche...

<u>Watch</u> - keep watching the victim(s) as they are carried downhill, paying particular attention to the last point you saw them

<u>DO NOT go for help!</u> - Sounds crazy but the victim only has a few minutes to breathe under the snow, so every second counts! Spend 30 minutes to an hour searching before going for help (unless you have a large party and someone can go while the rest search)

<u>Be aware</u> - assess the situation and dangers... in many cases it is safe to go in after the avalanche settles but proceed with caution!

<u>Look for clues</u> - start looking for any clues on the surface (like poles, a hand or foot, etc.) where victim was last seen. And remember, equipment and clothing can be ripped off during the avalanche but can help determine the direction they were carried.

<u>Switch to "receive"</u> - turn all transceivers to "receive" to try to locate a victim's signal (in the event victim is wearing one and has it set correctly!)

<u>Mark the spot</u> - if you lost sight of the victim or can't find any visible clues on the surface, mark the spot where victim was last seen

<u>Probe in a line</u> - when searching with probes, stand shoulder to shoulder in a line across the slope and repeatedly insert probes moving down the slope

<u>Listen</u> - make sure you listen for any muffled sounds as you search

<u>Find them...dig them out!</u> - if you find the victim, dig them out as quickly as possible! Survival chances reduce the longer they are buried.

To learn more about avalanches visit the North American Avalanche Centers' web site at <u>www.avalanche.org</u>. Or see our ADDITIONAL RESOURCES & WEB SITES listed at the end of this book.

Now we will briefly cover landslides and mudflows. Realize many types of disasters like earthquakes, volcanic eruptions, rain and wind erosion can cause land, rocks and mud to shift and move, sometimes at rapid speeds. Compound that with gravity and these earth movements can become extremely destructive.

Another major factor is the world's growing population is sprawling out of major cities and developing in high-risk areas. There are some warning signs to indicate if you have a potential problem.

LANDSLIDE WARNING SIGNS:

— cracks opening on hill slopes
— springs or saturated ground in areas not typically wet before
— evidence of slow, downhill movement of rock and soil
— tilted trees, poles, decks, patios or walls
— visible changes such as sags and bumps in the slope
— doors and windows sticking meaning structure may be shifting

Consult a professional landscaping expert for opinions and advice on landslide problems and what you can do to help slow it down or fix it.

BEFORE A LANDSLIDE OR MUDFLOW:

1. Ask your local emergency management office *(see Section 4 for State & Provincial listing)* if your property is a "landslide-prone" area. Or contact your County/Municipal or State/Provincial Geologist or Engineer.

2. Find out more about the **National Flood Insurance Program** (**NFIP**) since a mudflow is covered by their flood insurance policy *(see #8 in section BEFORE A FLOOD for more information on NFIP)*

3. Be prepared to evacuate and learn evacuation routes. *(see EVACUATION)*

4. Plant ground cover on slopes and build retaining walls.

DURING A LANDSLIDE OR MUDFLOW:

Whether you are in a vehicle, outside, or in your home – GET TO SAFER GROUND!

(Since most other disasters cause landslides and mudflows, we are not going to discuss this here but will cover it in their respective sections!)

AFTER A LANDSLIDE OR MUDFLOW:

<u>Listen</u> - local radio and TV reports will keep you posted on when it is safe to return or check with your local police or fire departments

<u>Insurance</u> - if your home suffers any damage, contact your insurance agent and keep all receipts for clean-up and repairs

What are <u>YOU</u> gonna do about...
AN EARTHQUAKE?

Earthquakes can cause buildings and bridges to collapse, down telephone and power lines, and result in fires, explosions and landslides. Earthquakes can also cause huge ocean waves, called tsunamis, which travel long distances over water until they hit coastal areas.

Our planet's surface is actually made up of slowly-moving sections (called "tectonic plates") that can build up friction or stress in the crust as they creep around. An earthquake occurs when this built up stress is suddenly released and transmitted to the surface of the earth by earthquake waves (called seismic waves).

There are actually about one million small earthquakes, or seismic tremors, per year around the world. Many earthquakes are too small to be felt, but when they happen, you will feel shaking, quickly followed by a rolling motion that can rotate up, down, and sideways that lasts from a few seconds to several minutes!

BEFORE AN EARTHQUAKE:

1. Review **EARTHQUAKE MITIGATION** tips on page 86.

2. Look for items in your home that could be hazardous during an earthquake.
   - Place large or heavy objects on lower shelves and fasten shelves to walls, if possible
   - Hang heavy pictures and mirrors away from beds
   - Store bottled foods, glass, china and other breakables on low shelves or in cabinets that can fasten shut
   - Repair any faulty electrical wiring and leaky gas connections

3. Know where and how to shut off electricity, gas and water at main switches and valves and share this information with family members.

4. Hold earthquake drills with your family
   - <u>SAFE SPOTS</u> - under a sturdy table or against an inside wall
   - <u>DANGER ZONES</u> - near windows or bookcases or furniture that can fall over

5. Sit down as a family and create an **Emergency Plan** and a **Disaster Supplies Kit** *(See Sections 1 and 3)*

6. Develop a plan for getting the family back together including out-of-state contacts to call to let everyone know you are okay.

7. Review your insurance policies. Some damage may be covered even without specific earthquake insurance.

DURING AN EARTHQUAKE:
Stay calm and stay where you are! Most injuries happen when people are hit by falling objects when running IN or OUT of buildings.

IF INDOORS – stay inside!
- Find a SAFE SPOT - under a heavy desk, bench or table or against an inside wall
- Avoid DANGER ZONES - glass, windows, outside door or walls and anything that can fall

IF OUTDOORS - stay outside! Try to move away from buildings, power lines and street lights.

IF IN A CROWDED PUBLIC PLACE - do not run for the door… a lot of other people will try to do that!
- Find a SAFE SPOT and avoid DANGER ZONES
- Move away from display shelves containing objects that will fall

IF IN A HIGH-RISE BUILDING – stay on the same floor!
- Find a SAFE SPOT (under a desk or table)
- Move away from outside walls and windows
- Stay in the building on the same floor since you may not have to evacuate
- Realize the electricity may go out and alarms and sprinkler systems may go on
- DO NOT use the elevators!

IF IN A MOVING VEHICLE - stop as quickly and safely as you can!
- Stay in the vehicle
- Try not to stop near or under buildings, trees, overpasses, or power lines
- Watch for road and bridge damage and be ready for aftershocks once you drive again

AFTER AN EARTHQUAKE:

<u>Aftershocks</u> - usually not as strong as an earthquake but can cause a lot more damage to weakened structures. Aftershocks can be just a few more shakes or may go on for days, months or even years!

<u>Injuries</u> - check for injuries to yourself and people around you. Do not try to move seriously injured people unless they are in danger. If you must move an unconscious (passed out) person, keep their head and neck still and call for help! *(See Section 2 – TIPS ON BASIC FIRST AID)*

<u>Light</u> - Never use candles, matches or lighters after an earthquake since there might be gas leaks. Use flashlights or battery powered lanterns.

<u>Check home</u> - look for structural damage and have a professional check it if anything seems strange

<u>Check chimney</u> - first check it from a distance to see if it looks normal and have a professional check it if anything seems strange - especially before using it!

<u>Clean up</u> - any flammable liquids (bleaches, gasoline, etc.) should be cleaned up immediately

<u>Inspect</u> - check all utility lines and appliances for damage
- **smell gas or hear hissing** - open a window and leave the building. Shut off main valve outside, if possible, and call a professional to turn it back on when it's safe
- **electrical damage** - switch off power at the main fuse box or circuit breaker
- **water pipes** - shut off the water supply at the main valve
- **toilets** - do not use until you know sewage lines are okay

<u>Water</u> - if water is cut off or contaminated then use water from your **Disaster Supplies Kit** or water heater

<u>Phones</u> - keep calls to a minimum to report emergencies since most lines will be down

<u>Listen</u> - keep up on news reports for the latest information

<u>Things to avoid:</u>
- **going out** - try to stay off the roads to reduce risk
- **watch out** - look out for fallen objects and bridge and road damage
- **stay away** - unless emergency crew, police or firemen ask for your help stay away from damaged areas
- **downed power wires**

<u>Tsunami</u> - If you live near the coast, a tsunami can crash into the shorelines so listen for warnings by local authorities *(see section on TSUNAMIS)*

<u>RED or GREEN sign in window</u> – After a disaster, Volunteers and Emergency Service personnel will be going door-to-door to check on people. By placing a sign in your window that faces the street near the door, you can let them know if you need them to **STOP HERE** or **MOVE ON**.

Either use a piece of RED or GREEN construction paper or draw a <u>big</u> RED or GREEN "X" (using a crayon or marker) on a piece of paper and tape it in the window.

- RED means STOP HERE!
- GREEN means EVERYTHING IS OKAY…MOVE ON!
- Nothing in the window would also mean STOP HERE!

What are <u>YOU</u> gonna do about...
AN EVACUATION?

Evacuations are more common than most people realize and happen for a number of reasons – fires, floods, hurricanes and chemical spills on the roads or railways.

When community evacuations become necessary, local officials provide information to the public through the media. Government agencies, the Red Cross and other disaster relief organizations provide emergency shelter and supplies. But as we have stated *several* times throughout this Manual, you should have enough food, water, clothing and emergency supplies for at least 3 days - or longer in a catastrophic disaster - in case you cannot be reached by relief efforts.

The amount of time to evacuate depends on the type of disaster, of course. Hurricanes can be tracked and allow a day or two notice to get ready, but many other types of disasters happen without much notice... so prepare NOW!!

BEFORE AN EVACUATION:
(Most of this is covered in Sections 1 & 3 of this manual.)

1. Ask your local emergency management office about community evacuation plans and learn the evacuation routes.

2. Sit down with your family and create an **Emergency Plan** and include where you would go and how you would get there *(see Section 1)*.

3. Include a place to meet your family in case you are separated from one another *(see EMERGENCY PLAN in Section 1)*.

4. Find out where your children will be sent if they are in school when an evacuation is announced.

5. Assemble a **Disaster Supplies Kit** *(see first part of Section 3)*.

6. Keep car fueled up if an evacuation seems likely since gas stations may be closed during emergencies.

7. Know how to shut off electricity, gas and water at main switches and valves (and have a wrench handy to do this.)

DURING AN EVACUATION:

Listen - keep up on news reports for the latest information

Supplies - Grab your **Disaster Supplies Kit** (water, food, clothing, emergency supplies, insurance and financial records, etc.)

What to wear - wear protective clothing and sturdy shoes

Secure home - close up and lock doors and windows, unplug appliances, protect water pipes (if freezing weather), etc. *(See specific disaster for additional tips on securing home)*

Shut off utilities - turn off the main water valve and electricity, if instructed to do so

Alert family/friends - let others know where you are going (or at least leave a message or note in clear view explaining where you can be found)

Things to avoid:
- **bad weather** - leave early enough so you are not trapped
- **shortcuts** - they may be blocked. Stick to the recommended Evacuation routes!
- **flooded areas** - roadways and bridges may be washed-out
- **downed power lines**

What are <u>YOU</u> gonna do about...
EXTREME HEAT?

What is Extreme Heat? Temperatures that hover 10 degrees or more above the average high temperature for that area and last for several weeks are considered "extreme heat" or a **heat wave**. Humid and muggy conditions can make these high temperatures even more unbearable. Really dry and hot conditions can cause dust storms and low visibility. **Droughts** occur when a long period passes without enough rainfall. A heat wave combined with a drought is a very dangerous situation!

Doing too much on a hot day, spending too much time in the sun or staying too long in an overheated place can cause **heat-related illnesses**. Know the symptoms of heat illnesses and be ready to give first aid treatment. *(see Section 2 HEAT-RELATED ILLNESSES)*

BEFORE EXTREME HEAT HITS:

1. Improve window air conditioners' performance:
    - Close any floor heat vents nearby
    - Insulate gaps around air conditioners (using foam, duct tape, etc.)
    - Use a circulating or box fan to spread the cool air around

2. Keep heat outside and cool air inside:
    - Use aluminum foil covered cardboard in windows to reflect heat back outside
    - Use weather-stripping on doors and windowsills to keep cool inside

3. Keep storm windows up all year to help keep cool in.

DURING EXTREME HEAT:

<u>Protect windows</u> - if you hang shades, drapes, sheets, or awnings on windows that get both morning and afternoon sun you can reduce heat from entering home by as much as 80%

<u>Conserve power</u> - during heat waves there are usually power shortages since everyone is trying to cool off, so stay indoors as much as possible.

<u>Conserve water</u> - lower water usage, especially during drought conditions. Watering the lawn or washing your car wastes precious water.

(Water Conservation Tip: put a brick in the **tank** of your toilet to reduce the amount of water used when you flush it.)

No A/C - if you have no air conditioning, try to stay on the lowest floor out of the sunshine and use electric fans to help keep you cool

Eat light - well-balanced light meals are best, especially fresh fruits and veggies!

Drink WATER - increase the amount of water you drink, especially in dry climates (deserts and high elevation) since you don't realize how dehydrated you are getting!

Limit booze - even though beer and alcoholic beverages may be refreshing on a hot day, they actually cause your body to dehydrate more!

What to wear - loose-fitting clothes that are light colored (to reflect heat)... and cover as much skin as possible. Dark colors attract sun and heat. Also wear a wide-brimmed hat to protect face and neck.

Use sunscreen - apply lotion or cream at least 20 minutes before going outside so the skin can absorb and protect, especially your face and neck (SPF 15-30 is best but an SPF 8 should be the lowest you go)! You usually burn within the first 10 minutes outside, so take care of your skin... especially children!! A sunburn slows the body's ability to cool itself and can be extremely dangerous.

Working outdoors - if you have to do yard work or other outdoor work, try to do it in the early morning hours to limit your exposure in the sun. The most powerful sun is between 10 a.m. and 3 p.m. (when you burn the quickest) so limit outdoor activity during the heat of the day, if possible.

Ozone alerts - these can cause *serious* danger to people with breathing and respiratory problems (especially children and the elderly) so limit your time outdoors when alerts are announced on the radio, newspapers or TV.

- **ozone** - a colorless gas that is in the air we breathe and is a major element of urban smog.
- **ground-level ozone** - considered an air pollutant and can lower resistance to colds, cause problems for people with heart and lung disease, and cause coughing and throat irritation
- **ozone levels** - (also called the Air Quality Index) between 0-50 are fine, but anything above 100 is extremely dangerous! When the weather is hot and sunny with little or no wind it can reach unhealthy levels.

What are <u>YOU</u> gonna do about...
FIRES & WILDFIRES?

Since fire spreads so quickly, there is NO time to grab valuables or make a phone call! In just <u>two</u> minutes a fire can become life threatening! In <u>five</u> minutes a house can be engulfed in flames!

A fire's heat and smoke are more dangerous than the actual flames since you can burn your lungs by inhaling the super-hot air. Fire produces a poisonous gas that makes you drowsy and disoriented (confused). Instead of being awakened by a fire, you could fall into a deeper sleep!

We are going to cover two subjects here -- **FIRES** and **WILDFIRES**. First we will discuss FIRES like you might encounter in your home or apartment, then we will cover WILDFIRES since there are many things people need to think about when living near wilderness areas.

BEFORE A FIRE (FIRE SAFETY TIPS):

1. **INSTALL SMOKE DETECTORS!** If you already have smoke detectors, clean and check them once a month and replace batteries once a year!

2. Create an Escape Plan that includes two escape routes from every room in the house and walk through the routes with your entire family. *(See Section 1 for checklists and Emergency Plans)* Also...
   - Make sure windows are not nailed or painted shut
   - Make sure security bars on windows have a fire safety opening feature so they can be easily opened from the inside... and teach everyone how to use it!
   - Teach everyone how to stay LOW to the floor (where air is safer) when escaping fire.
   - Pick a spot outside to meet family members after escaping a fire (meeting place).

3. Clean out storage areas and don't let newspapers and trash stack up!

4. Check electrical wiring and extension cords, and don't overload extension cords or outlets!

5. Never use gasoline or similar liquids indoors, and never smoke around flammable liquids!

6. Check furnaces, stoves, cracked or rusty furnace parts, and chimneys. They should all be clean and in working order.

7. Be careful with electrical space heaters and keep them at least 3 feet (1 m) away from flammable materials.

8. Make sure your home insulation does not touch electrical wiring.

9. Know where the circuit breaker box and gas valve is and how to turn them off, if necessary. (Always have a gas company representative turn on a main gas line.)

10. Install ABC fire extinguishers in the home and teach family members how to use them.

11. Ask your local fire department if they will inspect your home for fire safety and prevention.

12. Teach children that matches and lighters are TOOLS, not toys! And teach children if they see someone playing with fire they should tell an adult right away!!

13. Teach children how to report a fire and when to call 9-1-1.

DURING A FIRE:

Leave - DO NOT take time to try to grab anything except your family members! Once you are outside, do not try to go back in (especially for pets) - let the firemen do it!

GET DOWN - always stay low to the ground, especially if there is smoke around! Crawl on your hands and knees or squat down and walk like a duck… but keep moving to find a way out!

Closed door - Always feel the bottom of the door with the palm of your hand before you open it!
- **if door is cool** - leave quickly and crawl to an exit
- **if door is hot** – DO NOT open it and escape through a window, if possible

No way out - if you cannot find a way out of the room you are trapped in (door is hot and too high to jump) then hang a white or light-colored sheet outside the window to alert the firemen.

Use stairs - never take the elevator… always use stairs!

If YOU are on fire - if your clothes ever catch fire, **STOP** what you're doing, **DROP** to the ground, cover your face and **ROLL** until the fire goes out. Running only makes the fire burn faster!

Small fire - never try to put out a fire that is getting out of control since it may put you and your family in danger!

- **electrical fire** - do not use water… use a fire extinguisher approved for electrical fires
- **oil or grease fire in kitchen** - smother the fire with baking soda or salt (or if it's burning in a pan or skillet, carefully put a lid over it!)

AFTER A FIRE:

Don't go in there - never enter a fire-damaged building until the authorities say it is okay

Look - watch for signs of smoke or heat in case the fire isn't totally out

Utilities - have an electrician check your household wiring before you turn the power back on and DO NOT try to reconnect any utilities yourself!

Damage - look for structural damage (roof, walls, floors, etc.) since they may be weak

Call for help - your local disaster relief service (Red Cross, Salvation Army, etc.) can help provide shelter, food, or personal items that were destroyed.

Insurance - call your insurance agent and…
- Keep receipts of all clean-up and repair costs (for both insurance and income taxes)
- Do not throw away any damaged goods until an official inventory has been taken by your insurance company

If you rent - contact your landlord since it is the owner's responsibility to prevent further loss or damage to the site

Move your stuff - secure your personal belongings or move them to another location, if possible

To learn more about fire safety and fire prevention visit the U.S. Fire Administration's web site www.usfa.fema.gov or contact your local fire department, state or provincial emergency management official, or your insurance agent or representative.

Wildfires are intense fires that are usually caused by careless humans or lightning. Campfires, children playing with matches or lighters, and cigarettes are the probably the most common things that cause brush fires or wildfires so please be careful when you are out in the deserts, mountains, or any other heavy vegetation areas.

NEVER leave a campfire burning - make sure it is completely out using plenty of water before leaving the area. Stir the coals around with a stick or log while pouring water over them to ensure all the coals get wet and they are no longer hot. Any hot coals left unattended can be easily ignited by wind since they can stay hot for 24 - 48 hours!

When building a campfire, always choose a level site, clear away any branches and twigs several feet from the fire, and never build a fire beneath tree branches or on surface roots. Also, build at least 10 fcct (3 m) from any large rocks that could be blackened by smoke or cracked from the fire's heat. See your local Forest Service office or Ranger Station for more information on campfires and permits.

BEFORE A WILDFIRE (FIRE SAFETY TIPS):

1. Review **WILDFIRE MITIGATION** tips on pages 87-88.

2. Ask fire authorities or the forestry office for information on fire laws in your area.

3. Make sure that fire vehicles can get to your property and that your address is clearly marked.

4. Create a 30-100 ft (9-30 m) safety zone around your home (see tips on pages 87-88)

5. Teach children about fire safety and keep matches and lighters away from them.

6. Report hazardous conditions that could cause a wildfire.

7. Be prepared to evacuate.

DURING A WILDFIRE:

Listen - have a battery-operated radio available to keep up on news reports, weather and evacuation routes.

Evacuate? – if you are told to evacuate - do so immediately! *(see section on EVACUATION),* and <u>IF</u> you have time also…

- Secure your home - close windows, vents, doors, etc.
- Turn off utilities and tanks at main switches or valves, if instructed.
- Turn on a light in each room to increase the visibility of your home in heavy smoke.

<u>Head downhill</u> – remember fire climbs uphill since heat rises so always head down when evacuating the area

<u>Food & water</u> - if you prepared ahead, you will have your **Disaster Supplies Kit** handy to GRAB & GO… if not, gather up enough food and water for each family member for at least 3 days or longer!

<u>Be understanding</u> - please realize the firefighters main objective is getting wildfires under control and they may not be able to save every home! Try to understand and respect the firefighters and local officials decisions.

AFTER A WILDFIRE:

<u>Don't go in there</u> - never enter a fire-damaged area until the authorities say it is okay

<u>Look</u> - watch for signs of smoke or heat in case the fire isn't totally out

<u>Utilities</u> - have an electrician check your household wiring before you turn the power back on and DO NOT try to reconnect any utilities yourself!

<u>Damage</u> - look for structural damage (roof, walls, floors, etc.) since they may be weak

<u>Call for help</u> - your local disaster relief service (Red Cross, Salvation Army, etc.) can help provide shelter, food, or personal items that were destroyed.

<u>Insurance</u> - call your insurance agent and…

- Keep receipts of all clean-up and repair costs (for both insurance and income taxes)
- Do not throw away any damaged goods until an official inventory has been taken by your insurance company

<u>If you rent</u> - contact your landlord since it is the owner's responsibility to prevent further loss or damage to the site

<u>Move your stuff</u> - secure your personal belongings or move them to another location, if possible

What are <u>YOU</u> gonna do about... A FLOOD?

Floods are the most common natural disaster. Some floods develop over a period of several days, but a flash flood can cause raging waters in just a few minutes! Mudflows are another danger triggered by flooding that can bury villages without warning (especially in mountainous regions).

Everyone is at risk from floods and flash floods, even in areas that seem harmless in dry weather. Always listen to the radio or TV to hear the latest updates. Some other types of radios are the NOAA (National Oceanic and Atmospheric Administration) Weather Radio and Environment Canada's Weatheradio with battery backup and a tone-alert feature that will automatically alert you when a Watch or Warning has been issued.

BEFORE A FLOOD:

1. Review **FLOOD MITIGATION** tips on page 85.

2. Know the terms used to describe flooding:
   - **Flood watch** - flooding is possible
   - **Flash flood watch** - flash flooding is possible so move to higher ground if in a low-lying area
   - **Flood warning** - flooding is occurring or will occur soon and you may be told to evacuate so listen to the radio or TV for updates
   - **Flash flood warning** - flash flood is occurring so seek higher ground on foot immediately
   - **Urban and Small Stream Advisory** - flooding of small streams, streets and low-lying areas is occurring

3. Ask your local emergency management office *(see Section 1 for State & Provincial listings)* if your property is a "flood-prone" area. You may want to find out what elevation your property is so you can compare that level to flood levels announced by the radio and TV.

4. Also ask your local emergency office about the official flood warning signals and learn what to do when you hear them.

5. Find out if there are dams in your area and if they could be a hazard.

6. Be prepared to evacuate and learn your evacuation routes *(see EVACUATION)*.

7. Create an **Emergency Plan** and a **Disaster Supplies Kit** with your family *(see Sections 1 & 3)*

8. Know how to shut off the electricity, gas, and water at main switches

and valves and teach everyone how to do it!

9. Consider buying flood insurance - flood losses **are not** covered under homeowner's insurance policies! *(See page 85)* Flood insurance is available in the U.S. from the National Flood Insurance Program (NFIP) and there is a waiting period. (Homeowners, renters, and business owners in the U.S. can call NFIP at 1-800-427-4661 to learn more.) Canadians currently do not have a national flood program but contact your insurance representative with questions regarding coverage.

   Did you know...

   ... you can buy federal flood insurance through most major private insurance companies and licensed property insurance agents?!

   ... you do not have to own a home to have flood insurance as long as your community participates in the **NFIP**?!

   ... the **NFIP** offers coverage even if you live in a flood-prone area?!

   ... the **NFIP** offers basement and below ground level coverage?!

10. Ask your local building department or emergency management office how to "flood proof" your home.

11. Either videotape or take pictures of your home and personal belongings and store them in a safe place (like a fireproof box or a safety deposit box) along with important papers.

DURING A FLOOD (OR HEAVY RAIN):

Be aware - listen to local news reports and watch for flash floods especially if you are near streams, drainage channels and areas known to flood

Get on higher ground - if you are in a low-lying area, get to higher ground

Prepare to evacuate – *(see section on EVACUATION)*, but also...
- Secure your home and move important items to upper floors
- Turn off utilities at main switches or valves if instructed by authorities and DO NOT touch electrical equipment if you are wet or standing in water!
- Fill up your car with fuel.

Obey warnings - If road signs, barricades, or cones are placed in areas - OBEY THEM! Most areas have fines for people who ignore these posted warnings, especially if they get stuck or flooded! DO NOT drive around these barricades... find another way to get where you are going!

Things to avoid:

- **moving water** - 6 inches (15 cm) of moving water can knock you off your feet and 2 ft (.6 m) of moving water will float a car!
- **flooding car** - if flood waters rise around your car, get out and move to higher ground if you can do it safely! (Don't try to walk through moving water!)
- **bad weather** - by leaving early enough so you are not trapped
- **flooded areas** - roadways and bridges may be washed-out
- **downed power lines** - extremely dangerous in floods!!

AFTER A FLOOD (OR HEAVY RAIN):

Things to avoid:

- **flood waters** - stay away from flood waters since it may be contaminated by oil, gasoline or raw sewage or may be electrically charged from underground or downed power lines - wait for local authorities to approve returning to flooded areas
- **moving water** - 6 inches (15 cm) of moving water can knock you off your feet and 2 ft (.6 m) of moving water will float a car!
- **flooded areas** - roadways and bridges may be washed-out or weakened
- **downed power lines** - extremely dangerous and report them to the power company

Obey warnings - If road signs, barricades, or cones are placed in areas - OBEY THEM! Most areas have fines for people who ignore these posted warnings, especially if they get stuck or flooded! DO NOT drive around these barricades... find another way to get where you are going!

Snakes - watch out for snakes in areas that were flooded

Flooded food - throw away food that has come into contact with flood waters since eating it can make you sick!

Drinking water - wait for officials to advise when water is safe to drink!

Wash your hands - wash hands often with clean water and soap since flood waters are dirty and full of germs!

Use bleach – the best thing to use for cleaning up flooded areas is household bleach since it will help kill germs

Listen - continue listening to your battery-powered radio for updates on weather and tips on getting assistance for housing, clothing, food, etc.

Insurance - call your insurance agent to see if you're covered for flooding

What are <u>YOU</u> gonna do about...
HAIL STORMS?

Hail is the largest form of precipitation that begins as tiny ice pellets and grows by colliding with supercooled water droplets as it gets tossed around violently in strong updraft winds. As the pellet continues to be tossed, it builds layer by layer until it becomes so heavy that it drops out of the sky as hailstones.

Hailstone diameters can range from 1/16 of an inch to 5 inches (2 mm to 13 mm) - basically meaning they can range in size from tiny pebbles to golfballs to grapefruits or softballs! The largest hailstone ever recorded in the U.S. weighed 1.67 pounds and 17.5 inch (44 cm) in circumference!

Hail is usually present in powerful storms like tornadoes, thunderstorms and even some winter storms mainly due to the strong winds and rapidly rising air masses needed to form hailstones.

Hail occurs across Canada but more frequently happens in the Canadian Prairies (particularly the Calgary-Medicine Hat area). This region can expect up to 10 hail storms a year and most of the damaging hailstorms generally occur from May to October. The U.S. averages about 3,000 hail storms each year across the country and a majority of the storms occur between March and June.

The worst hailstorm in Canadian history hit Calgary, Alberta in September 1991. The 30-minute downpour caused almost $400 million in insurance claims devastating crops, property and livestock. In 1996 Alberta started a hail suppression program using aircraft that fly over developing storms and seed clouds with silver iodide particles to reduce the size of the hailstones.

BEFORE A HAIL STORM:

Since hail storms are pretty localized events, it is difficult to prepare for "hail", however please review the other topics that create hail storms (Thunderstorms, Tornadoes and Winter storms) to learn what to do and how to protect yourselves during these events!

1. Listen for local radio or TV weather forecasts and updates.

2. If possible, secure your vehicles in a garage or under substantial covering.

3. Bring pets and livestock in to some type of shelter for their safety.

4. Stay inside until the entire storm system passes.

DURING A HAIL STORM:

<u>Listen</u> - listen to the radio or TV for more information for updates on weather conditions and other types of warnings

IF INDOORS – stay inside until the storm passes and don't try to go out and protect your property!

IF OUTDOORS - take shelter under the strongest structure you can find (especially if hailstones are large!)

IF IN A VEHICLE - carefully pull over to the shoulder and seek shelter under an overpass or the closest substantial structure available

AFTER A HAIL STORM:

<u>Listen</u> - continue listening to the radio or TV for updates on weather

<u>Check it out</u> - check for damage to trees and shrubs because if they are damaged, your roof is most likely damaged too. Also check your vehicles and structures for damage but don't put yourself in danger if storms are still active!

<u>Cover it up</u> - cover up holes in your roof and broken windows in your car and home to keep water out

<u>Insurance</u> - Call your insurance agent to set up a visit to your home or to take your vehicle down for inspection

What are <u>YOU</u> gonna do about...
HAZARDOUS MATERIALS?

Chemical plants are one source of hazardous materials, but there are many others that exist in both industries and homes. There are about 38,000 hazardous materials waste sites in the U.S. and many communities have a Local Emergency Planning Committee (LEPC) that keeps local planners, companies and members of the community informed of potential risks.

We [the public] should all learn more about hazardous materials and how they can affect our lives.

BEFORE A HAZARDOUS MATERIALS DISASTER:

1. Ask your local fire department about emergency warning procedures:

   - **Outdoor warning sirens or horns** - ask what they mean and what to listen for
   - **Emergency Alert System (EAS)** - information and alerts via TV and radio
   - **"All-call" telephoning** - an automated system for sending recorded messages via telephone
   - **Residential route alerting** - messages announced from vehicles equipped with public address systems (loud speakers on top of car or van)

2. Ask your Local Emergency Planning Committee (LEPC) or emergency management office about community plans for responding to hazardous materials accident at a plant or a transportation accident involving hazardous materials.

3. Ask your LEPC where large quantities of extremely hazardous substances are stored and where they are used.

4. Use the LEPC's information to see if you and your family are at risk - especially if you are close to freeways, railroads, or factories which produce or transport toxic waste.

5. Arrange a neighborhood tour of industries that produce or transport toxic waste and include neighbors, local officials and the media.

6. Be prepared to evacuate *(see EVACUATION section)*.

DURING A HAZARDOUS MATERIALS DISASTER:

Call for help - if you see a hazardous materials accident, call 9-1-1, the local emergency number, or the fire department

Listen - listen to the radio or TV for more information, especially if you hear a warning signal

IF INDOORS – stay inside!
- Close your windows
- Seal gaps under doorways and windows with wet towels and duct tape
- Turn off A/C, fans, and vents so no air is drawn in from the outside

IF OUTDOORS - stay upstream, uphill, or upwind from the disaster since hazardous materials can be carried by wind and water quickly. Try to get at least ½ mile or kilometer away or as far away as possible!

IF IN A VEHICLE - close your windows and shut off the vents to reduce the risk!

Stay away - get away from the accident site to avoid contamination

Evacuate? - if you are told to evacuate… do so immediately! If officials say you have time, close windows, shut vents and turn off attic fans. *(see EVACUATION section)*

What to wear - keep your body fully covered and wear gloves, socks and shoes (even though these may not keep you totally safe, it will help!)

Things to avoid:
- **chemicals** - spilled liquid materials, airborne mist, or solid chemical
- **contaminated food or water** - do not eat or drink any food or water that may have been exposed to the hazardous materials

AFTER A HAZARDOUS MATERIALS DISASTER:

Don't go home - until local authorities say it is safe!

<u>Air out</u> - open windows, vents and turn on fans in your home

<u>Listen</u> - keep up with local reports from either the radio or TV

<u>Clean up</u> - a person or item that has been exposed to a hazardous chemical could spread it

- **decontamination** - follow instructions from local authorities since it depends on the chemical. You may need to shower or rinse off items or you may be told to stay away from water - so check first!
- **strange symptoms** - if unusual symptoms show up, get to a hospital or a medical expert right away! Remove any contaminated clothing and put on fresh, loose, warm clothing and listen to local reports on the radio.
- **store shoes & clothes** - put exposed clothing and shoes in tightly sealed containers without touching other materials and call local authorities to ask how to get rid of them
- **tell people you've been exposed** - tell everyone who comes in contact with you that you may have been exposed to a toxic substance!
- **land and property** - ask local authorities how to clean up your land or property

<u>Strange vapors or danger</u> - report any strange vapors or other dangers to the local authorities immediately.

What are <u>YOU</u> gonna do about…
HURRICANES, CYCLONES & TYPHOONS?

Hurricane season in North America is generally between June and November. Hurricanes are tropical cyclones with torrential rains and winds of 74 - 155 miles per hour (120 - 250 km/h) or faster. These winds blow in a counter-clockwise direction (or clockwise in the Southern Hemisphere) around a center "eye". The "eye" is usually 20 to 30 miles (32 to 48 km) wide, and the storm may be spread out as far as 400 miles (640 km)!

As the hurricane approaches the coast, a huge dome of water (called a storm surge) will crash into the coastline. Nine out of ten people killed in hurricanes are victims of storm surge! Hurricanes can also cause tornadoes, heavy rains and flooding.

What's with all the different names?

You may have heard different words used to describe different storms depending on where you live in the world. It's very confusing, but hopefully we can help explain all the different names… and hopefully we don't make any weather specialists angry!

<u>Cyclone</u> - an atmospheric disturbance with masses of air rapidly rotating around a low-pressure center… (sort of like a dust devil or a tornado)

<u>Tropical Depression</u> - maximum surface winds of less than 39 miles per hour (62 km/h) over tropical or sub-tropical waters with storms and circular winds

<u>Tropical Storm</u> - the tropical cyclone is labeled a Tropical Storm if winds are between 39-73 mph (62 - 117 km/h) and given a name to track it

<u>Hurricane, Typhoon, Tropical cyclone</u> - surface winds are higher than 74 mph (120 km/h)… and depending on where it is happening will determine what it is called!

Where in the world do they use these names?
(Please note: We are only listing a <u>few</u> major countries or areas for each!)

<u>Cyclone</u> - used in several parts of the world - **Indian Ocean, Australia, Africa, SW and southern Pacific Ocean**

<u>Hurricane</u> - used in the North Atlantic Ocean, the Northeast Pacific Ocean (east of the dateline), or the South Pacific Ocean (east of 160) - **both**

coasts of North America, Puerto Rico, Caribbean Islands, and Central America

Typhoon - used in the Northwest Pacific Ocean west of the dateline - **Guam, Marshall Islands, Japan, Philippines, Hong Kong, coastal Asia**

Tropical cyclone - used in the Southwest Pacific Ocean west of 160E or most of the Indian Ocean - **Australia, Indonesia, Madagascar, Africa, Middle East**

Hurricanes are classed into five categories based on their wind speeds, central pressure, and damage potential:

Category One – winds 74-95 mph (120-153 km/h)
Category Two – winds 96-110 mph (153-177 km/h)
Category Three – winds 111-130 mph (177-209 km/h)
Category Four – winds 131-155 mph (209-250 km/h)
Category Five – winds are greater than 155 mph (250 km/h)

BEFORE A HURRICANE:

1. Review **WIND, FLOOD, & LIGHTNING MITIGATION** tips on pages 83 - 87.

2. Know the terms used to describe hurricanes:
   - **Hurricane watch** - a hurricane is possible within 36 hours so listen to TV and radio for updates
   - **Hurricane warning** - a hurricane is expected within 24 hours. You may be told to evacuate (if so, leave immediately) and listen to the radio or TV for updates

3. Listen for local radio or TV weather forecasts and updates. (Some other radios available are Environment Canada's Weatheradio and NOAA's Weather Radio with battery backup and a tone-alert feature that automatically alert you when a Watch or Warning has been issued.)

4. Ask about evacuation plans and if your neighborhood will be told to evacuate. *(see section on EVACUATION)*

5. Create an **Emergency Plan** and a **Disaster Supplies Kit** with your family, especially for the Elderly & Disabled. *(see Sections 1 & 3)*

6. Know how to shut off the electricity, gas, and water at main switches and valves and teach family members how to do it!

7. Make plans to protect your property with storm shutters or board up windows with plywood that is measured to fit your windows. Tape does not prevent windows from breaking! *(See pages 83-85 for tips)*

8. Consider getting flood insurance... well in advance since there is a waiting period! *(see pages 85 & 112 for information on NFIP)*

9. Make a record of your personal property using either a video camera or photographs.

DURING A HURRICANE WATCH OR WARNING:

Listen - have a battery-operated radio available to keep up on news reports and evacuation routes.

Evacuate? – if you are told to evacuate - do so immediately! *(see section on EVACUATION)*, but if you have time also...

- Secure your home - close storm shutters or put up boards on windows, moor your boat, and secure outdoor objects or put them inside since winds will blow them around.
- Turn off utilities at main switches or valves, if instructed.
- Fill up your car with fuel.

Food & water - if you prepared ahead, you will have your **Disaster Supplies Kit** handy to GRAB & GO... if not, gather up enough food and water for each family member for at least 3 days!

Pets - make arrangements for your pets since most shelters will not allow pets *(see Section 1 or call the Humane Society)*

Things to avoid:
- **moving water** - 6 inches (15 cm) of moving water can knock you off your feet and 2 ft (.6 m) of moving water will float a car!
- **flooding car** - if flood waters rise around your car, get out and move to higher ground if you can do it safely! (Don't try to walk through moving water!)
- **bad weather** - leave early enough so you are not trapped
- **flooded areas** - roadways and bridges may be washed-out
- **downed power lines** - extremely dangerous in floods!!

Stay indoors - if you do not evacuate, stay indoors and stay away from windows. A lull in the storm could only be the "eye" and winds can start again! Listen to radio or TV reports.

<u>Limit phone calls</u> - only use the phones in an emergency so it keeps the lines open for local authorities!

AFTER A HURRICANE:

<u>Stay put</u> - stay where you are if you are in a safe location and don't return home (if you've been evacuated) until local authorities say it's okay

<u>Listen</u> - continue listening to your battery-powered radio for updates on weather and tips on getting assistance for housing, clothing, food, etc.

<u>Stick together</u> - Keep the family together since this is a very stressful time and try to find chores for the children so they feel like they are helping with the situation.

<u>Things to avoid</u>:
- **flood waters** - stay away from flood waters since it may be contaminated by oil, gasoline or raw sewage or may be electrically charged from underground or downed power lines - wait for local authorities to approve returning to flooded areas
- **moving water** - 6 inches (15 cm) of moving water can knock you off your feet and 2 ft (.6 m) of moving water will float a car!
- **flooded areas** - roadways and bridges may be washed-out or weakened
- **downed power lines** - extremely dangerous and report them to the power company

<u>Flooded food</u> - throw away any food that has come into contact with flood waters since eating it can make you sick!

<u>Drinking water</u> - wait for officials to advise when water is okay to drink!

<u>Wash your hands</u> - wash hands often with <u>clean</u> water and soap

<u>Use bleach</u> – the best thing to use for cleaning up flooded areas is household bleach since it will help kill germs

<u>Insurance</u> - call your insurance agent to set up a visit to your home

<u>RED or GREEN sign in window</u> – After a disaster, Volunteers and Emergency Service personnel should be going door-to-door to check on people. By placing a sign in your window that faces the street near the door, you can let them know if you need them to STOP HERE or MOVE ON (if your home is still standing!). Either use a piece of RED or GREEN construction paper or draw a <u>big</u> RED or GREEN "X" (using a crayon or

marker) on a piece of paper and tape it in the window.

- RED means STOP HERE!
- GREEN means EVERYTHING IS OKAY…MOVE ON!
- Nothing in the window would also mean STOP HERE!

Donations – lots of people want to help victims of a hurricane and here are some tips…

- **Wait & see** - do not donate food, clothing or other personal items unless they are specifically requested
- **Money** - donations to a known disaster relief group, like the Red Cross, is always helpful
- **Volunteers** - if local authorities ask for your help, bring your own water, food and sleeping gear

What are <u>YOU</u> gonna do about...
A NUCLEAR POWER PLANT EMERGENCY?

The World Nuclear Association reports as of early 2002 over 430 nuclear power reactors in 31 countries produce over 16 percent of the total electricity generated worldwide.

There are over 100 commercial power plants in the U.S. (in most states across the country) and 20 power stations in Canada (18 in Ontario, 1 in Quebec and 1 in New Brunswick) meaning millions of citizens live within 10 miles (16 km) of an operating plant.

Even though national governments and associations monitor and regulate the construction and operation of these plants, accidents are possible and do happen.

An accident could result in dangerous levels of radiation that could affect the health and safety of the public living near the nuclear power plant, as well as people up to 200 miles (320 km) away depending on winds and weather -- meaning millions and millions of North Americans could potentially be affected!

How is radiation detected?
You cannot see or smell radiation - scientists use special instruments that can detect even the smallest levels of radiation. If radiation is released, authorities from Federal and State or Provincial governments and the utility will monitor the levels of radioactivity to determine the potential danger so they can protect the public.

What is the most dangerous part of a nuclear accident?
Radioactive iodine - nuclear reactors contain many different radioactive products, however, the most dangerous product is iodine which, once absorbed, concentrates on the thyroid. The greatest population that will suffer in a nuclear accident is **children** (including <u>unborn</u> children) since their thyroid is extremely active, but all people are at risk of absorbing radioactive iodine.

How can I be protected from radioactive iodine?
Potassium iodide (KI) - can be purchased over-the-counter now and is known to be an effective thyroid-blocking agent. In other words, it fills up the thyroid with good iodine that keeps the radioactive iodine from being absorbed into our bodies.

What if I am allergic to iodine?

According to the United States Nuclear Regulatory Commission Office of Nuclear Material Safety and Safeguards, the FDA suggests that risks of allergic reaction to potassium iodide are minimal compared to subjecting yourself to cancer from radioactive iodine. You may want to ask your doctor or pharmacist what you should keep on hand in the event of an allergic reaction.

Many European countries stockpile potassium iodide (KI), especially since the Chernobyl incident. Several states within the U.S. are considering or already have stockpiles of KI ready in case of a nuclear power plant accident as part of their Emergency Planning.

Community Planning for Emergencies

Local, state and provincial governments, Federal agencies and the electric utilities have developed emergency response plans in the event of a nuclear power plant accident.

U.S. plans define two "emergency planning zones" (EPZs).

- **Plan One** - covers a 10-mile (16 km) radius from nuclear plant where it is possible people could be harmed by direct radiation exposure

  NOTE: People within this 10-mile (16 km) radius are regularly given emergency information about radiation, evacuation routes, special arrangements for the handicapped, contact names and other materials (usually through brochures, phone books, utility bills, etc.)

- **Plan Two** - covers usually up to a 50-mile (80 km) radius from the plant where accidentally released radioactive materials could contaminate water supplies, food crops and livestock

Canada's Provincial Nuclear Emergency Plans define three "zones". *(Per Ontario Ministry of Public Safety & Security EMO PNEP Backgrounder)*

- **Contiguous Zone** - extends approximately 3 kilometres from the nuclear facility

- **Primary Zone** - extends approximately 10 kilometres from the nuclear facility site

- **Secondary Zone** - extends approximately 50 kilometres from the nuclear facility

3 Ways to Reduce Radiation Exposure

DISTANCE - the more distance between you and the source of radiation, the less radiation you will receive so that's why in a serious nuclear accident you are told to evacuate!

SHIELDING - heavy, dense materials between you and radiation is best so this is why you want to stay indoors since the walls in your home should be good enough to protect you (in some cases… so listen to radio and TV to see if you need to evacuate!)

TIME - most radioactivity loses its strength rather quickly so by limiting your time near the source of radiation it reduces the amount you receive.

Please note: Another type of accident involving possible nuclear radiation exposure may be a "weapon of mass destruction" or WMD. This topic is briefly covered in the next section called **TERRORISM**. The below may be useful in the event of a nuclear WMD event so please review both sections, but always listen to local authorities since they will provide instructions to the public for that specific incident.

Before a Nuclear Power Plant Emergency:

1. Know the terms used to describe a nuclear emergency: **U.S. / (Canada)**
    *   **Notification of Unusual Event / (Reportable Event)** - a small problem has occurred at the plant. No radiation leak is expected. Federal, state/provincial and county/municipal officials will be told right away. No action on your part will be necessary.
    *   **Alert / (Abnormal Incident)** - a small problem has occurred, and small amounts of radiation could leak inside the plant. This will not affect you. You should not have to do anything.
    *   **Site Area Emergency / (Onsite Emergency)** - a more serious problem… small amounts of radiation could leak from the plant. If necessary, officials will act to ensure public safety. Area sirens may be sounded and listen to your radio or TV for information.
    *   **General Emergency / (General Emergency)** - the MOST serious problem… radiation could leak outside the plant and off the plant site. The sirens will sound so listen to local radio or TV for reports. State/Provincial and county/municipal officials will act to assure public safety and be prepared to follow their instructions!
2. Learn your community's warning system and pay attention to "test" dates so you can find out if you can HEAR the sirens! Nuclear power

plants are required to install sirens and other warning devices to cover a 10-mile (16 km) area around the plant. (If you live outside the 10-mile [16 km] area you will probably learn of the event through your local TV and radio stations so just be aware that winds and weather can impact areas as far as 200 miles [320 km] away!!)

3. Ask the power company that operates the nuclear power plant for brochures and information (which they or government sends automatically to people within a 10-mile [16 km] radius of the plant).

4. Learn the emergency plans for schools, day cares, nursing homes or other places your family may be and find out where they will go if there is an evacuation.

5. Be prepared to evacuate! *(see section on EVACUATION)*

DURING A NUCLEAR POWER PLANT EMERGENCY:

<u>Stay calm</u> - not all accidents release radiation and may be contained to the plant only!

<u>Listen</u> - to your radio or TV for updates! Local authorities will give specific instructions and information… pay attention to what THEY tell you rather than what is written in this Manual since they know the facts for that specific accident!

<u>Leave if</u>… - evacuate only if you are told to do so by local authorities.
- Grab your **Disaster Supplies Kit** *(see Section 3)*
- Close and lock home doors and windows and close fireplace damper
- Close car windows and vents and use "re-circulating" air while in the car.
- Keep listening to radio for evacuation routes and instructions.

<u>As long as you are NOT told to evacuate, do the following…</u>

IF INDOORS - you are not told to evacuate, stay inside!
- Close doors and windows and your fireplace damper.
- Turn off air conditioner, ventilation fans, furnace and other air intakes (that pull in air from outside)
- Go to a basement or underground area (if possible).
- Keep a battery-operated radio with you to hear updates.
- Stay inside until authorities tell you it is safe to go out!

IF OUTDOORS - Get indoors as soon as possible!
- Cover your mouth and nose with a cloth or handkerchief.
- Once inside, remove clothing, take a good shower and put on fresh clothing and different shoes. Put the clothes and shoes you were wearing in a plastic bag, seal it and store it out of the way! Local authorities can tell you what to do with them.

IF IN A VEHICLE - keep windows up, close vents, use "recirculating" air and listen to radio for updates.

Food - put food in covered containers or in the refrigerator, and any food that was not in a covered container should be washed first

Pets & livestock - get them indoors or in shelters with clean food and water that has not been exposed to air-borne radiation (food and water that has been stored), especially milk-producing animals

Take your iodine - IF radioactive iodine has been released into the air from the power plant accident, some states *may* decide to provide KI pills (mentioned at the beginning of this section) to people in a 10-mile radius. This is at the option of state and local government unless you prepare in advance and keep KI handy for such emergencies.

(NOTE: Take iodine ONLY as directed by state, provincial or local public health authorities and follow instructions on the package exactly!)

AFTER A NUCLEAR POWER PLANT EMERGENCY:

Listen - continue to listen to local radio and TV for updates

Gardens – local authorities will provide information concerning the safety of farm and homegrown products. You may want to check with your agricultural extension agent for more information.

Crops - unharvested crops are hard to protect but crops that are already harvested should be stored inside, if possible.

Wash & peel - vegetables and fruits that were not already harvested should be washed and peeled before using, but you should check with local officials to confirm if they are safe

Milk - local emergency officials should inspect milk from cows and goats before using

What are <u>YOU</u> gonna do about...
TERRORISM?

Terrorism is the use of force or violence against persons or property usually for emotional or political reasons or for ransom. Some terrorists try to convince people that their government is powerless to prevent terrorism and use threats to create public fear so they get publicity for their cause.

Most people don't want to think about this type of accident or event and we are not trying to say you need to panic - just be aware that these types of things happen. There is really nothing you can do to prevent most types of terrorism, but you should learn about the various types.

One type of terrorism that we <u>can</u> help prevent is the use of guns and bombs by children and youth against other groups of children at schools. A key solution to stopping this type of violence is through communication, education and awareness – and it starts within <u>the FAMILY</u>!

The Federal Bureau of Investigation categorizes terrorism in two ways:

<u>Domestic terrorism</u> - terrorist activities are directed at certain groups or parts of the government within the U.S. without foreign direction

> Some examples of domestic terrorism include the recent shootings and bomb threats at schools, the Oklahoma City bombing of the Federal Building, and the letters mailed to various groups with a white powdery substance inside (anthrax scares).

<u>International terrorism</u> - terrorist activities are foreign-based by countries or groups outside the U.S.

> Some examples of international terrorism include bombings like the U.S.S. Cole in Yemen and U.S. Embassies in other countries, the incidents at the Pentagon and the World Trade Center, hostage situations with civilians and military personnel in various countries, or threats with weapons of mass destruction.

Most of the terrorist attacks we hear about involve bombs, guns, kidnappings and hijackings, but another form of terrorism includes <u>biological</u>, <u>chemical</u> or nuclear agents used as <u>weapons of mass destruction</u>.

Biological agents - infectious microbes (tiny life forms) or toxins used to produce illness or death in people, animals or plants and can be inhaled or swallowed (such as anthrax)

Chemical agents - poisonous gases, liquids or solids that can kill or slow down or weaken people, destroy livestock or crops and can be absorbed through the skin or inhaled (such as mustard gas or nerve gas).

In either a chemical or biological attack, the local authorities will instruct the public on what to do and any exposure to either agent requires immediate attention with professional medical staff!

Weapons of mass destruction (WMD) - chemical, biological, radiological, or nuclear weapons *(see pages 124-128 for tips on nuclear accidents)*. In the event of a terrorist threat against North America with WMD, there are officials from all levels of government responsible for employing and equipping WMD terrorism response units to manage the situation. It is critical the general public listen to officials' instructions.

*Please see **APPENDIX C** to review a "County Emergency Preparedness Terrorism Emergency Operations Outline" contributed by South Carolina's Charleston County Emergency Preparedness Department. *

BEFORE A TERRORIST ATTACK:

BE AWARE! - you should always be aware of your surroundings!

Stay current on alerts - Canada's OCIPEP *(pages 164-167)* and U.S.'s Office of Homeland Security *(APPENDIX A)* post alerts on the Internet.

Know the targets - terrorists usually pick targets that bring very little damage to themselves and areas that are easy to access by the public (like international airports, government buildings, major events, schools, etc.)

Things to watch out for:
- **unknown packages** - DO NOT accept a package or case from a stranger
- **unattended bags** - DO NOT leave your bags or purses alone (especially when traveling) and NEVER ask strangers to watch your stuff!
- **emergency exits** - always be aware of where Emergency EXITS are… just casually look around for the signs since most are marked well in public places

Bomb Threat - could be received on the telephone or in the mail

- If you ever receive a bomb threat, get as much information from the caller as possible.
- Try to keep them on the telephone as long as you can and write down <u>everything</u> that is said! (Since you will be nervous or scared, your notes will be very helpful!)
- Notify the police and the building management.
- Stay away from any strange packages - don't touch anything!
- Evacuate the building, keep the sidewalks clear and stay away from windows.

NOTE: It is too difficult to know exactly what to do **DURING** and **AFTER** a terrorist attack since there are so many kinds and many unknowns, so we are just focusing on a "bomb" disaster in a building according to information from FEMA. During ANY type of terrorist attack listen to local officials instructions on the radio or TV and follow their instructions without any hesitation!!

DURING A BUILDING EXPLOSION:

<u>Get out</u> - get out of the building as quickly and calmly as possible!

<u>Things to watch out for</u>:
- **Falling objects** - if things are falling off bookshelves or from the ceiling, get under a sturdy table or desk
- **Fire** - stay low to the floor (crawl or walk like a duck)
  Only use the stairs (do not use elevators)!
  Check doors before opening (If <u>HOT</u>, DO NOT open - find another exit!)

AFTER A BUILDING EXPLOSION:

<u>If you are trapped in an area:</u>
- **light** - use a flashlight, if you have one – don't use matches or lighters in case of gas leaks
- **be still** - try to stay still so you won't kick up dust
- **breathing** - cover your mouth with a piece of clothing
- **make noise** - tap on a pipe or wall so rescuers can hear you (shout only as a last resort since it can cause you to inhale dangerous amounts of dust)

<u>Rescuing others</u> - untrained persons should not try to rescue people who are inside a collapsed building… wait for emergency personnel to arrive – then, if they need you, they will ask!

What are <u>YOU</u> gonna do about...
A THUNDERSTORM?

Thunderstorms are very common... in fact, at any given moment, nearly 1,800 thunderstorms can be in progress over the face of the earth! The U.S. usually averages about 100,000 thunderstorms each year.

Lightning always comes with a thunderstorm since that is what causes thunder! If you have ever heard someone say lightning never strikes the same place twice... WRONG... it can! In fact, lightning OFTEN strikes the same place several times during one storm. Lightning actually comes from the ground up into the air and back down - we just see it as it comes down so it looks like it's coming from the clouds. Severe thunderstorms can also bring heavy rains, flooding, hail, strong winds, tornadoes and microbursts (a sudden vertical drop of air)!

BEFORE A THUNDERSTORM:

1. Review **WIND, FLOOD, & LIGHTNING MITIGATION** tips on pages 83 - 87.

2. Know the terms used to describe major thunderstorms:
   - **Severe Thunderstorm Watch** - severe thunderstorms are possible
   - **Severe Thunderstorm Warning** - severe thunderstorms are occurring

3. If you hear thunder, you are close enough to the storm to be struck by lightning. Get to safe shelter immediately!

4. Unplug appliances, if possible (even if you have a surge protector) and it's wise to move the plug away from the outlet.

DURING A THUDERSTORM:

Listen to battery operated radio for local reports on the storm (especially severe storms which can cause tornadoes!)

IF INDOORS - stay inside until the storm passes.
   - <u>telephone</u> - it is best not to use the telephone since phone lines can conduct electricity
   - <u>don't shower</u> - it sounds weird, but it is best to avoid taking a bath or shower since the water can carry an electrical charge if lightning strikes near your home

IF OUTDOORS - try to get to safe shelter quickly.
- Move away from tall things (trees, towers, fences, telephone or power lines) since they attract lightning.
- If you are surrounded by trees while outside, take shelter under the <u>shorter</u> trees
- Get to a low lying area (like a ditch or a valley), but watch out for flash floods
- Stay away from metal things (umbrellas, baseball bats, bicycles, fishing rods, wire fences, etc) since they can attract lightning
- **Be small** - make yourself a small target by crouching down and put your hands on your knees (and do not lie flat on the ground since that makes you a bigger target!)

IF IN A BOAT - get to land and to shelter quickly! Water is extremely dangerous when there's lightning!

IF IN A VEHICLE - keep windows closed and stay out of a convertible, if possible (mainly because the top is usually fabric and that could make you the highest target if lightning strikes!)

<u>Hairy sign</u> - if you feel your hair stand on end and feel tingly (which means lightning is about to strike)… crouch down and bend forward putting your hands on your knees (be small)! Do not lie flat on the ground… it makes you a bigger target!

<u>If someone is struck by lightning:</u>
- the victim does not carry electrical charge and CAN be touched safely
- call 9-1-1 or your local EMS (emergency) telephone number
- victim will have 2 wounds - an entrance and an exit burn and give first aid if needed *(see ELECTRICAL BURNS)*

AFTER A THUNDERSTORM:

<u>Things to avoid:</u>
- **flooded areas** – stay away from flood waters since it may be contaminated by oil, gasoline or raw sewage or may be electrically charged from underground or downed power lines or lightning – wait for authorities to approve returning to flooded areas
- **moving water** – 6 inches (15 cm) of moving water can knock you off your feet and 2 ft (.6 m) of moving water will float a car!
- **storm-damaged areas**
- **downed power lines**

What are <u>YOU</u> gonna do about...
A TORNADO?

The U.S. has more tornadoes than anywhere else in the world, with sightings in all 50 states. Canada is # 2 in volume of tornadoes and has several high risk areas including Alberta, southern Ontario, southwestern Quebec and a band across southern Saskatchewan and Manitoba to Thunder Bay, Ontario. British Columbia and western New Brunswick are also tornado zones.

Most injuries or deaths caused by tornadoes are from collapsing buildings, flying objects or trying to outrun a twister in a vehicle. Tornadoes can also produce violent winds, hail, lightning, rain and flooding.

Did you know...

     ... tornadoes can produce wind speeds as high as 311 mph (500 km/h), move across the ground at speeds up to 75 mph (120 km/h), and reach as high as 40,000 feet (12,200 m) above the ground?!

     ... the U.S. has more tornadoes than any other place in the world and averages 1,000 tornado sightings each year?!

     ... heavy items (like pieces of roof) can be thrown for many miles and lighter objects (like a piece of paper) can be scattered up to 200 miles (320 km) away?!

     ... the force of a tornado can rip the bark off trees, tear clothes off people, and pluck the feathers off chickens?!

BEFORE A TORNADO:

1. Review **WIND, FLOOD, & LIGHTNING MITIGATION** tips on pages 83 - 87.

2. Know the terms used to describe tornado threats:
   - **Tornado watch** - a tornado is possible so listen to your TV or radio for updates
   - **Tornado warning** - a tornado has been sighted so take shelter immediately and keep a battery operated radio with you for updates
   - **Severe Thunderstorm Watch** - severe thunderstorms are possible
   - **Severe Thunderstorm Warning** - severe thunderstorms are occurring

3. Ask your local emergency management office *(see Section 4)* or your local Red Cross chapter about the tornado threat in your area.

4. Also ask your local emergency office about the community warning signals and learn what to do when you hear them.

5. Always have a battery-operated radio with extra batteries so you can hear any alerts.

6. Know what county or area you live in so you can listen for that name on the radio updates.

7. Find the best place to seek shelter underground (like a basement, a safe room or storm cellar). If you don't have underground shelter, then the next best place is in the middle section of the building or a hallway on the lowest floor or a bathroom or closet.

8. Know the locations of shelters in places where you and your family spend time (schools, nursing homes, buildings, etc.)

9. Practice going to your shelter with your family and "duck and cover" (use your hands and arms to protect your head and stay down low).

10. Either videotape or take pictures of your home and personal belongings and store copies of them and other important papers in a place away from your home (like a safety deposit box).

DURING A TORNADO:

<u>Listen</u> - to local news reports on a battery-operated radio for updates on tracking the twister

<u>Take cover</u> - wherever you are, if you hear or see a tornado coming, take cover immediately!

IF IN A TRAILER OR MOBILE HOME – GET OUT!!!
* get to a stronger shelter... or ...
* stay low to the ground in the nearest dry ditch or culvert with your hands covering your head.
* If you hear or see water in the ditch, move quickly to a drier spot in case lightning strikes nearby.

IF INDOORS - get to a safe place right away!
* <u>In house or small building</u> - go to basement or storm cellar or get to a room in the middle of the building on the lowest floor (like a

bathroom, closet, or hallway) and get under something sturdy (like a table) and stay there until the danger has passed! If possible, put a mattress or heavy covers over you to help protect you!

- In a school, nursing home, hospital, factory or shopping center - go to the designated shelter areas (or interior hallways on the lowest floor) and stay away from windows and open areas.

- In a high-rise building - go to a small, interior room or hallway on the lowest floor possible and avoid windows.

IF OUTDOORS - try to take shelter in a nearby basement or sturdy building! If you cannot get indoors, LIE FLAT in a dry ditch, ravine or culvert with your hands covering your head. (If you hear or see water, move quickly to drier spot in case lightning strikes nearby!)

IF IN A VEHICLE - GET OUT and take shelter in a building or lie flat in a ditch with your hands covering your head! DO NOT try to out-drive a tornado! You never know which direction a tornado is going to go since it can change directions and it moves too fast!

AFTER A TORNADO:

Watch out - look for broken glass and downed power lines

Injured people - do not try to move injured people unless they are in danger and call for help immediately

Don't go in there - try to stay out of buildings or homes that are damaged until it is safe to enter and wear sturdy work boots and gloves

What are <u>YOU</u> gonna do about...
A TSUNAMI?

A tsunami (pronounced soo-nam'-ee) is a series of huge, destructive waves caused by an undersea disturbance from an earthquake, volcano, landslide, or even a meteorite. As the waves approach the shallow coastal waters, they appear normal and the speed decreases. Then, as the tsunami nears the coastline, it turns into a gigantic, forceful wall of water that smashes into the shore with speeds exceeding 600 miles per hour (965 km/h)! Usually tsunamis are about 30 feet (9 m) high but extreme ones can be as high as 100 feet (30 m)!

A tsunami is a series of waves and the first wave may <u>not</u> be the largest one, plus the danger can last for many hours after the first wave hits. During the past 100 years, more than 200 tsunamis have been recorded in the Pacific Ocean alone and Japan has suffered a majority of them due to earthquakes.

Did you know...

> ... a tsunami is <u>not</u> a tidal wave since it has nothing to do with the tide?!
> ... another name used to describe a tsunami is "harbor wave" since "tsu" means harbor and "nami" means wave in Japanese?!
> ... sometimes the ocean floor is exposed near the shore since a tsunami can cause the water to recede or move back before slamming in to shore?!
> ... boats, rocks and other debris can be moved inland hundreds of feet with massive power that can destroy everything in its path?!
> ... tsunamis can travel up streams and rivers that lead to the ocean?!

BEFORE A TSUNAMI:

1. Review **WIND and FLOOD MITIGATION** tips on pages 83 - 85.

2. Listen to tsunami warnings - they mean a tsunami exists! Pay attention to local reports on TV or radio and do what officials say for your own safety!

3. If near the water, watch for a noticeable rise or fall in the normal depth of coastal water, which is an advance warning of a tsunami.

4. If you feel an earthquake in the Pacific Coast area (from Alaska down to Baja), listen to the radio for tsunami warnings.

5. Don't be fooled by the size of one wave - more will follow... a small tsunami at one beach can be a giant wave a few miles away!

6. Be ready to evacuate *(see section on EVACUATION)*

DURING A TSUNAMI:

Leave - if you are told to evacuate, DO IT! Remember - a tsunami is a series of waves and the first one may be small but who knows what the rest will bring!

IF ON A SHORE - Get off the shore and get to higher ground immediately! Stay away from rivers and streams that lead to the ocean! You cannot outrun a tsunami and once you see the wave, it's too late!

IF ON A BOAT - it depends where you are... either get to land or go further out to sea!

- in port - you may not have time to get out of the port or harbor and out to sea so check with authorities to see what you should do (smaller boats may want to dock and get to land quickly)

- in open ocean - DO NOT return to port if a tsunami warning has been issued since the wave action is barely noticeable in the open ocean! Stay out in the open sea or ocean until authorities advise the danger has passed.

AFTER A TSUNAMI:

Listen - whether you are on land or at sea, local authorities will advise when it is safe to return to the area so listen to radio and TV updates

Watch out - look for downed power lines, flooded areas and other damage caused by the waves

Don't go in there - try to stay out of buildings or homes that are damaged until it is safe to enter and wear sturdy work boots and gloves when working in the rubble

Strange critters – be aware that the waves may bring in many critters from the ocean (marine life) so watch out for pinchers and stingers!

RED or GREEN sign in window – After a disaster, Volunteers and Emergency Service personnel may be going door-to-door to check on people. By placing a sign in your window that faces the street near the door, you can let them know if you need them to STOP HERE or MOVE ON. Either use a piece of RED or GREEN construction paper or draw a big RED or GREEN "X" (using a crayon or marker) on a piece of paper and tape it in the window.

- RED means STOP HERE!
- GREEN means EVERYTHING IS OKAY…MOVE ON!
- Nothing in the window would also mean STOP HERE!

What are <u>YOU</u> gonna do about...
A VOLCANO?

A volcano is a mountain that opens downward to a reservoir of molten rock (like a huge pool of melted rocks) below the earth's surface. Unlike mountains, which are pushed up from the earth's crust, volcanoes are formed by their buildup of lava, ash flows, and airborne ash and dust. When pressure from gases and the molten (melted) rock becomes strong enough to cause an explosion, it erupts and starts to spew gases and hot rocks through the opening.

Volcanic eruptions can hurl hot rocks for at least 20 miles (32 km) and eruptions can cause sideways blasts, lava flows, hot ash flows, landslides, mudflows, and avalanches. They can also cause earthquakes, thunderstorms, flash floods, wildfires, and tsunamis!

Fresh volcanic ash, made of crushed or powdery rock, can be acidic (to burn), gritty, glassy and smelly. Lung damage to small infants, older people or people with breathing problems can be caused by the combination of the burning gas and ash.

Sometimes volcanic eruptions can drive people from their homes forever.

Did you know...
>   ... more than 80 percent of the Earth's surface above and below sea level was formed by volcanic eruptions?!
>   ... there are more than 850 active volcanoes around the world and more than two-thirds of them are part of the "Ring of Fire" (a region that encircles the Pacific Ocean)?!
>   ... volcanic eruptions can impact our global climate since they release gases like sulfer and carbon dioxide into the earth's atmosphere?!
>   ... the primary danger zone around a volcano covers about a 20-mile (32 km) radius?!
>   ... floods, airborne ash or dangerous fumes can spread 100 miles (160 km) or more?!
>   ... a pyroclastic flow is an avalanche of ground-hugging hot rock, ash and gas that races down the slope of a volcano at speeds of 60 mph (97 km/h) with temperatures of nearly 1,300 degrees Fahrenheit (704 degrees Celsius)?!
>   ... Alaska has over 40 active volcanoes?!

BEFORE A VOLCANIC ERUPTION:

1. Review the **MITIGATION** tips on pages 83 - 88.

2. Learn about your community's warning systems and the evacuation routes, and be prepared to follow their instructions.

3. Develop an **Emergency Plan** and have a **Disaster Supplies Kit** ready in case of evacuation or disaster *(see Sections 1 & 3)*. (NOTE: You may want to include goggles or safety glasses and masks for each family member in your Kit to protect their eyes and lungs from ash!)

4. Avoid visiting volcanoes unless authorities have approved safe viewing sites.

DURING A VOLCANIC ERUPTION:

<u>Listen</u> - do what local authorities say, especially if they say evacuate!

<u>Leave</u> - if you are told to evacuate, DO IT! Don't think you are safe to stay at home and watch the eruption... the blast can go for many, many miles and can cause wildfires and many other hazards!

<u>Watch out</u> - eruptions cause many other disasters...

- **flying rocks** - rocks can be hurled for miles at extremely fast speeds!
- **mudflows or landslides** - they can move faster than you can walk or run
- **lava flows** - burning liquid rock and nothing can stop it
- **gases and ash** - try to stay upwind since winds will carry these and they are harmful to your lungs
- **fires** - hot rocks and hot lava will cause buildings and forests to burn

IF INDOORS - stay inside but be aware of ash, rocks, mudflows or lava!

- Close all windows, doors, and dampers to keep out ash fall
- Bring pets inside (and if time permits, move livestock into closed shelters)
- Listen for creaking on your rooftop (in case ash flow gets too heavy and could cause it to collapse!)

IF OUTDOORS - try to get indoors, if not…

- Try to stay upwind so the ash and gases are blown away from you
- Watch for falling rocks and if you get caught in a rockfall, roll into a ball to protect your head!
- Get to higher ground and avoid low-lying areas since poisonous gases can collect there and flash floods could happen
- Use a dust-mask or a damp cloth over face to help breathing, wear long-sleeved shirts and pants, and use goggles or safety glasses to protect your eyes

IF IN A VEHICLE - try to avoid driving unless it is absolutely required.

- Slow down and keep speed down to 35 mph (56 km/h) or slower, especially because of thick dust
- Shut off your engine if you leave your car and park in garage, if possible (to reduce the amount of ash from getting in it)
- Look upstream before crossing a bridge in case a mudflow or landslide is coming

AFTER A VOLCANIC ERUPTION:

<u>Listen</u> - local authorities will say when it is safe to return to the area (especially if you had to evacuate) and give any other updates

<u>Water</u> - check with local authorities before using water, even if there was just ash fall (since the gases and ash can contaminate water reserves)

<u>What to wear</u> - if you must be around the ash fall, you should wear long sleeve shirts, pants, sturdy boots or shoes, gloves and keep your mouth and nose covered with a dust-mask or damp cloth

<u>Ash</u> - remove ash buildup from rooftops and rain gutters since it is very heavy and be careful when you are around ash since it is bad for your lungs

What are <u>YOU</u> gonna do about...
WINTER STORMS & EXTREME COLD?

Winter storms can last for many days and include high winds, freezing rain, sleet or hail, heavy snowfall and extreme cold. These types of winter storms can shut down a city or area mainly due to blocked roads and downed power lines. People can be stranded in their car or trapped at home for hours or days, but there are many other hazards that come with these storms.

The leading cause of death during winter storms is automobile or other transportation accidents and the second leading cause of death is heart attacks. Hypothermia (or freezing to death) is very common with the elderly who sometimes die inside their homes because it is so cold.

The best way to protect yourself from a winter disaster is to plan ahead before the cold weather begins. Take advantage of spring sales when winter items are cheaper so you are ready for next winter!

BEFORE A WINTER STORM:

1. Review **WIND** and **WINTER STORM MITIGATION** tips on pages 83 - 89.

2. Know the terms used to describe winter conditions:
   - **Freezing rain** - rain that freezes when it hits the ground, creating a coating of ice on the roads and walkways
   - **Hail** - rain that turns to ice while suspended and tossed in the air from violent updrafts in a thunderstorm
   - **Sleet** - rain that turns to ice pellets before reaching the ground (which can cause roads to freeze and become slippery)
   - **Winter Weather Advisory** - cold, ice and snow are expected
   - **Winter Storm Watch** - severe winter weather such as heavy snow or ice is possible within a day or two
   - **Winter Storm Warning** - severe winter conditions have begun or are about to begin
   - **Blizzard Warning** - heavy snow and strong winds will produce a blinding snow, near zero visibility, deep drifts and life-threatening wind chills
   - **Frost/Freeze Warning** - below freezing temperatures are expected

3. Put together emergency supplies along with a **Disaster Supplies Kit** *(see Section 3)* and <u>add</u> the following items at home for winter storms:

- **rock salt** - good for melting ice on walkways
- **sand or kitty litter** - to improve traction
- **emergency heating equipment and fuel** - good to have a backup in case power is cut off
  <u>Fireplace</u> - gas fireplace or a wood burning stove or fireplace
  <u>Generator</u> – gas or diesel models available
  <u>Kerosene heaters</u> – ask you Fire Department if they are LEGAL in your community and ask about safety tips in storing fuel!
  <u>Charcoal</u> - NEVER use charcoal indoors since the fumes are deadly in a contained room but it's fine for using outdoors!!
- **extra wood** - keep a good supply in a dry area
- **extra blankets** – either regular blankets or emergency blankets (about the size of a wallet)

4. Make sure your home is "winterized" (see tips on pages 88-89)

DURING A WINTER STORM:

<u>Listen</u> - get updates from radio and TV weather reports

<u>What to wear</u> - dress for the season…

- **layer** - it is much better to wear several layers of loose-fitting, light-weight, warm clothing than one layer of heavy clothing (and the outside garment should be waterproof)
- **mittens** - mittens are warmer than gloves
- **hat** - most of your body heat is lost through the top of your head
- **scarf** - cover your mouth with a scarf or wrap to protect your lungs from the cold air

<u>Don't overdo it</u> - be careful when shoveling snow or working outside since the cold can put added strain on your heart and cause a heart attack (even in children!)

<u>Watch for signs</u> - playing or working out in the snow can cause exposure so look for signs of…

- **Frostbite** - loss of feeling in your fingers, toes, nose or ear lobes or they turn really pale
- **Hypothermia** - you start to shiver a lot, slow speech, stumbling, or feel very tired… in either case, get inside quickly and get medical help!

WINTER DRIVING TIPS

Driving - If you must travel, consider taking public transportation. If you must drive, travel during the day, don't travel alone, and let someone know where you are going. Stay on the main roads and avoid taking back roads.

Winterize car - Make sure you have plenty of antifreeze and snow tires (or chains or cables at least). Keep your gas tank as full as possible during cold weather.

Winter Kit - Carry a "winter" car kit in the trunk *(see CAR KIT in Section 3)* and also throw in...

- **warm things** – mittens, hat, emergency blanket, sweater, waterproof jacket or coat
- **cold weather items** - windshield scraper, bag of road salt or sand
- **emergency items** - brightly colored cloth or distress flag, booster cables, emergency flares, tow chain or rope
- **miscellaneous** - (food, water, etc. is mentioned in **CAR KIT**)

Stranded - if you get trapped in your car by a blizzard or break down...

- **get off the road** - if you can drive, pull the car off the main road onto the shoulder
- **hazard lights** - turn on your hazards and hang a bright cloth or distress flag on the antenna
- **stay in car** - stay inside until help arrives (your **CAR KIT** will provide food and water and other comforts if you planned ahead!)
- **start your car** - turn on the car's engine for about 10 minutes each hour (open a window slightly for ventilation of fumes) and run the heater and turn on the dome light (while it is running)
- **if you walk** - if you do walk away from your car, make sure you can see the building or shelter (no more than 100 yards or 10 m)
- **exercise** - DO NOT overdo it, but light exercises can help keep you warm
- **sleeping** - if you are not alone, take turns sleeping so someone can watch for rescue crews
- **exhaust pipe** - check the exhaust pipe now and then and clear out any snow

AFTER A WINTER STORM:

Restock - stock up on any items you used right after the storm clears so you are ready for the next one!

TIPS ON SHELTER LIVING
DURING AN EMERGENCY

Taking shelter during a disaster could mean you have to be somewhere for several hours or possibly several days or weeks! It could be as simple as going to a basement during a tornado warning or staying home without electricity or water for several days during a major storm.

In many emergencies, the Red Cross and other organizations set up public shelters in schools, city or county buildings and churches. While they often provide water, food, medicine, and basic sanitary facilities, you should plan to have your own supplies - especially water *(see Section 3 for* ***DISASTER SUPPLIES KIT)***.

No matter where you are or whom you are with, you should use the following tips while staying in a shelter during an emergency:

<u>Don't leave</u> - stay in your shelter until local authorities say it's okay to leave. Realize that your stay in your shelter can range from a few hours to two weeks according to FEMA! In some cases it might even be longer!

<u>Take it outside</u> - restrict smoking to well-ventilated areas (outside if it is safe to go out) and make sure the smoking materials are disposed of safely!

<u>Behave</u> - living with many people in a confined space can be difficult and unpleasant but you must cooperate with shelter managers and others in the shelter

<u>24-hour watch</u> - take turns listening to radio updates and keep a 24-hour communications and safety watch going

<u>Toilet</u> - bathrooms may not be available so make sure you have a plan for human waste *(see Section 3-TIPS ON SANITATION OF HUMAN WASTE)*

<u>Pets</u> - public shelters do not allow pets due to health reasons so you will have to make arrangements to keep them somewhere else. (You can try the Humane Society or local Animal Shelter - if they are still functioning after a disaster!)

Tips on Recovering From A Disaster

Unless you have been in a disaster before, it is hard to imagine how you will handle the situation. Coping with the human suffering and confusion of a disaster requires a certain inner strength. Disasters can cause you to lose a loved one, neighbor or friend or cause you to lose your home, property and personal items. The emotional effects of loss and disruption can show up right away or may appear weeks or months later.

We are going to briefly cover "emotional" recovery tips then cover some "general" recovery tips on what to do AFTER a disaster. Remember -- people *can* and *do* recover from all types of disasters, even the most extreme ones, and you <u>can</u> return to a normal life.

Emotional Recovery Tips – Handling Emotions

Since disasters usually happen quickly and without warning, they can be very scary for both adults and children. They also may cause you to leave your home and your daily routine and deal with many different emotions, but realize that a lot of this is normal human behavior. It is very important that you understand no matter what the loss is… there is a natural grieving process and every person will handle that process differently.

Some general reactions to disasters:

<u>Right after disaster</u> – shock, fear, disbelief, hard time in making decisions, refusing to leave home or area, finding help or helping others

<u>Days, weeks or months after disaster</u> – anger or moodiness, depression, loss of weight or change in appetite, nightmares, crying for "no reason", isolation, guilt, anxiety, domestic violence

<u>Additional reactions by children</u> - thumb sucking, bed-wetting, clinging to parent(s) or guardian, won't go to bed or school, tantrums (crying or screaming), problems at school

Please note: If any of your disaster reactions seem to last for quite some time, please seek professional counseling to help deal with the problem. There is nothing wrong with asking for help in recovering emotionally!

Tips for Adults & Kids

<u>Deal with it</u> - recognize your own feelings so you can deal with them properly and responsibly

TALK - talking to others helps relieve your stress and helps you realize you are not alone... other victims are struggling with the same emotions... especially your own family! And don't leave out the little kids... let them talk about their feelings and share your feelings with them.

Accept help - realize that the people who are <u>trying</u> to help you <u>want</u> to help you so please don't shut them out or turn them away!

Time out - whenever possible, take some time off and do something you enjoy to help relieve the stress... and do something fun with the whole family like a hike, a picnic or play a game.

Rest - listen to your body and get as much rest as possible. Stress can run you down so take care of yourself and your family members.

Slow down - Don't feel like you have to do everything at once and pace yourself with a <u>realistic</u> schedule.

Stay healthy - Make sure everyone cleans up with soap and <u>clean</u> water after working in debris. Also, drink lots of clean water and eat healthy meals to keep up your strength.

Work out - physical activity like running or walking is good to release energy and stress

Hug - a hug or a gentle touch (holding a hand or an arm) is very helpful during stressful times

Be an example - kids look to adults during a disaster so your reactions will impact the kids (meaning if you act alarmed or worried – they will be scared, if you cry – they cry, etc.)

Stick together - keep the family together as much as possible and include kids in discussions and decisions when possible

Draw a picture - ask your kids to draw a picture of the disaster to help you understand how he or she views what happened

Explain - calmly tell your family what you know about the disaster using facts and words they can understand and tell everyone what will happen next so they know what to expect

Reassurance - let your kids and family know that they are safe and repeat this as often as necessary to help them regain their confidence

Praise - recognizing good behavior and praise for doing certain things (even the littlest of things) will help boost the morale

Watch your temper - stress will make tempers rise but don't take out your anger on others, especially kids. Be patient and control your emotions.

Let kids help - including your kids in small chores during the recovery and clean up processes will help them feel like they are part of the team and give them more confidence

Let others know - work with your kids' teachers, day-care staff, babysitters and others who may not understand how the disaster has affected them

GENERAL RECOVERY TIPS - AFTER A DISASTER
RETURNING TO A DAMAGED HOME:

Listen - keep a battery-operated radio with you for any emergency updates

What to wear – wear sturdy work boots and gloves

Check outside first - before you go inside, walk around the outside to check for loose power lines, gas leaks, and structural damage

Call a professional - if you have any doubts about the safety of your home, contact a professional inspector

Don't go in there - if your home was damaged by fire, do not enter until authorities say it is safe (also don't enter home if flood waters remain around the building)

Use a flashlight - there may be gas or other flammable materials in the area so use a battery-operated flashlight (do not use oil, gas lanterns, candles or torches and do not smoke!)

Watch out - look out for animals, especially snakes (flooding will carry them) and use a stick to poke through debris

Things to check - some things you want to do first…
- Check for cracks in the roof, foundation and chimneys
- Watch out for loose boards and slippery floors
- Check for gas leaks (either by smell or listen for a hissing or blowing sound)
  - Start with the hot water heater
  - Turn off the main gas valve from outside
  - Call the gas company
- Check the electrical system (watch for sparks, broken wires or the smell of hot insulation)
  - Turn off the electricity at the main fuse box or circuit breaker
  - DO NOT touch the fuse box, circuit breaker or wires if in water or you are wet!

- Check appliances <u>after</u> turning off electricity at main fuse and if wet, unplug and let them dry out. Call a professional to check them before using
- Check the water and sewage system and if pipes are damaged, turn off the main water valve
- Clean up any spilled medicines, bleaches or gasoline
- Open cabinets carefully since things may fall out
- Look for your valuable items (jewelry and family heirlooms) and protect them
- Try to patch up holes, windows and doors to protect your home from further damage
- Clean and <u>disinfect</u> everything that got wet (bleach is best) since mud left behind by floodwaters can contain sewage and chemicals.
- If your basement is flooded, pump it out slowly (about 1/3 of the water per day) to avoid damage since the walls may collapse if the surrounding ground is still waterlogged
- Check with local authorities about the water since it could be contaminated! Wells should be pumped out and the water tested before using, too
- Throw out food, makeup and medicines that may have been exposed to flood waters and check refrigerated foods to see if they are spoiled. If frozen foods have ice crystals then okay to refreeze
- Call your insurance agent, take pictures of the damage, and keep ALL receipts on cleaning and repairs

GETTING HELP: DISASTER ASSISTANCE

<u>Listen</u> - local TV and radio announce where to get emergency housing, food, first aid, clothing and financial assistance after a disaster

<u>Help finding family</u> - The Red Cross maintains a database to help you find your family members, but <u>please</u> do not contact the Red Cross office in the disaster area since they will be swamped!

<u>Agencies that help</u> - The Red Cross is often stationed right at the scene of a disaster to help people with their immediate medical, food and housing needs. Some other sources of help include the Salvation Army, church groups and synagogues and various other Social Service agencies from local, state and provincial governments.

<u>President declares a "Major Disaster" (U.S.)</u> - in severe disasters, the government (FEMA) steps in and provides people with the following:
- Temporary housing
- Counseling

- Low interest loans and grants
- Businesses and farms are also eligible for aid through FEMA.

FEMA's Disaster Application Centers - FEMA will set Centers up at local schools and municipal buildings to manually process applications or they can be taken over the telephone. (The FEMA phone number will be announced by local TV and radio reports.)

I lost my job (in U.S.) - People who lose their job due to the disaster may apply for weekly benefits using Disaster Unemployment Assistance. You should call your local unemployment office or 1-800-462-9029 (TTY: 1-800-462-7585) for registration information.

Legal help (in U.S.) - local members of the American Bar Association Young Lawyers Division offer free legal counseling to low-income individuals after the President declares a major disaster. (FEMA can provide more information at their Disaster Centers or you can call 1-800-525-0321 for assistance.)

Canadian disaster - In the event of a large-scale disaster in Canada, the provincial or territorial government pays out money to individuals and communities in accordance with its provincial disaster assistance program. *(Federal assistance - Disaster Financial Assistance Arrangements [DFAA] is paid to the province or territory... not to individuals and communities as FEMA does in the U.S.!)*

Recovering financially - the American Red Cross and FEMA developed the following list to help you minimize the financial impact of a disaster

- **First things first** - 1) remove valuables only if your residence is safe to enter, 2) try to make temporary repairs to limit further damage, and 3) notify your insurance company immediately!
- **Conduct an inventory** - make sure you get paid for what you lost
- **Reconstruct lost records** - use catalogs, want ads, Blue Books, court records, request old tax forms from the IRS, escrow papers, etc. to help determine value of lost possessions
- **Notify creditors and employers** - let the people you do business with know what has happened
- **File an insurance claim** - get all policy numbers; find out how they are processing claims; identify your property with a sign; file claims promptly, work with adjusters, etc.
- **Obtain loans and grants** - find out if you qualify for emergency financial assistance from the local media reports
- **Avoid contractor rip-offs** - get several estimates; don't rush into anything; ask for proof of licenses, permits and insurance; get

contract in writing; never prepay; get a signed release of lien; check out the contractor with the local Better Business Bureau, etc.

- **Reduce your tax bite** - you may be eligible for tax refunds or deductions but know they can be very complex so you may want to ask an expert for advice

* Note: A detailed brochure called "Recovering Financially After a Disaster" prepared by the National Endowment for Financial Education®, the Red Cross, and FEMA is available on the Red Cross's web site or may be at your local Red Cross chapter. (see Section 4)

MITIGATION (REDUCING THE IMPACT FOR THE NEXT TIME)

The last thing you want to think about after a disaster is "what if it happens again"! Before you spend a lot of time and money repairing your home after a disaster, you should find ways to avoid or reduce the impact of the next disaster.

FEMA recommends the following mitigation tips AFTER A DISASTER:

1. Ask your local building department about agencies that purchase property in areas that have been flooded. You may be able to sell your property to a government agency and move to another location.

2. Determine how to rebuild your home to handle the shaking of an earthquake or high winds. Ask your local government, a hardware dealer or a private home inspector for technical advice.

3. Consider the options for flood-proofing your home. Determine if your home can be elevated to avoid future flood damage.

4. Make sure all construction complies with local building codes that pertain to seismic, flood, fire and wind hazards. Make sure the roof is firmly secured to the main frame of the house. Make sure your contractors know and follow the codes. Make sure construction is inspected by a local building inspector.

For more information about mitigation, please see pages 83-90.

TIPS ON HELPING OTHERS
IN THEIR TIME OF NEED

A disaster really brings out the generosity of many people who want to help the victims. Unfortunately, sometimes this kindness overwhelms agencies that are trying to coordinate relief efforts so please use the following general guidelines defined by FEMA on helping others after a disaster.

1. In addition to the people you care for on a daily basis, consider the needs of your neighbors and people with special needs.

2. If you want to volunteer your services immediately after a disaster, listen to local news reports for information about where volunteers are needed. Until volunteers are specifically requested, stay away from disaster areas.

3. If you are needed in a disaster area, bring your own food, water and emergency supplies. This is especially important in cases where a large area has been hit since these items may be in short supply.

4. Do not drop off food, clothing or any other item to a government agency or disaster relief organization unless a particular item has been requested. They usually don't have the resources to sort through the donations and it is very costly to ship these bulk items.

5. If you wish, give a check or money order to a recognized disaster relief organization like the Red Cross. They can process the funds, purchase what is needed and get it to the people who need it most. Your entire donation goes towards the disaster relief since these organizations raise money for overhead expenses through separate fund drives.

6. If your company wants to donate emergency supplies, donate a quantity of a given item or class of items (such as nonperishable food) rather than a mix of different items. Also, determine where your donation is going, how it's going to get there, who's going to unload it and how it will be distributed. Without good planning, much needed supplies will be left unused.

TIPS FOR VOLUNTEERS
AND DISASTER WORKERS

FEMA offers excellent information for disaster workers and volunteers to help them recover emotionally and physically <u>after</u> <u>helping</u> with a disaster.

They also coordinate many counseling programs to help you adjust back to your normal life since the images and emotions can take weeks or months - even years - to heal.

Please DO NOT hold these feelings and emotions inside since they can lead to emotional destruction of you and your loved ones through domestic violence, divorce, isolation, addiction and/or suicide.

Please take advantage of these programs and counselors offered by FEMA following a disaster. There is absolutely nothing wrong with asking for some help in recovering emotionally.

Section 4

Organizations' Emergency Contact Names & Numbers

ABOUT THE AMERICAN RED CROSS:

Extracted from the American Red Cross Disaster Services web site:

The mission of American Red Cross Disaster Services is to ensure nationwide disaster planning, preparedness, community disaster education, mitigation, and response that will provide the American people with quality services delivered in a uniform, consistent, and responsive manner.

The American Red Cross responds to disasters such as hurricanes, floods, earthquakes, and fires, or other situations that cause human suffering or create human needs that those affected cannot alleviate without assistance. It is an independent, humanitarian, voluntary organization, not a government agency.

All Red Cross assistance is given free of charge, made possible by the generous contribution of people's time, money, and skills.

CONTACTING YOUR LOCAL AMERICAN RED CROSS:

There are a few different ways of finding your local Red Cross Chapter:

If you have access to the Internet, you can check their web site

http://www.redcross.org

On the left hand side of the screen is a place to type in your zip code and click on FIND button

… or …

You can browse through a list of local American Red Cross websites by clicking on the link shown below the zip code box on the web site

… or …

Check your local telephone book in the white pages under BUSINESS LISTINGS for the American Red Cross!

Write in their number here for future reference:

Your Local American Red Cross Address:

_____

Telephone #: _____

About the Federal Emergency Management Agency (FEMA):

The Federal Emergency Management Agency - FEMA - is an independent agency of the federal government, reporting to the United States President. Since its founding in 1979, FEMA's mission has been clear:

to reduce loss of life and property and protect our nation's critical infrastructure from all types of hazards through a comprehensive, risk-based, emergency management program of mitigation, preparedness, response and recovery.

FEMA Regional Offices

FEMA Region I
(serving CT, MA, ME, NH, RI, VT)
J.W. McCormack POCH
Room 442
Boston, MA 02109-4595
(617) 223-9540 FAX 617 223-9519
www.fema.gov/regions/i/index.shtm

FEMA Region II
(serving NJ, NY, PR, VI)
26 Federal Plaza, Suite 1307
New York, NY 10278-0001
(212) 680-3600 FAX 212 680-3681
www.fema.gov/regions/ii/index.shtm

FEMA Region III
(serving DC, DE, MD, PA,VA, WV)
One Independence Mall
615 Chestnut Street, 6th Floor
Philadelphia, PA 19106-4404
(215) 931-5608 FAX 215 931-5621
www.fema.gov/regions/iii/index.shtm

FEMA Region IV
(serving AL, FL, GA, KY, MS, NC, SC, TN)
3003 Chamblee Tucker Road
Atlanta, GA 30341
(770) 220-5200 FAX 770 220-5230
www.fema.gov/regions/iv/index.shtm

FEMA Region V
(serving IL, IN, MI, MN, OH, WI)
536 South Clark St., 6th Floor
Chicago, IL 60605
(312) 408-5500 FAX 312 408-5234
www.fema.gov/regions/v/index.shtm

FEMA Region VI
(serving AR, LA, NM, OK, TX)
Federal Regional Center
800 North Loop 288
Denton, TX 76209-3698
(940) 898-5399 FAX 940 898-5325
www.fema.gov/regions/vi/index.shtm

FEMA Region VII
(serving IA, KS, MO, NE)
2323 Grand Boulevard, Suite 900
Kansas City, MO 64108-2670
(816) 283-7061 FAX 816 283-7582
www.fema.gov/regions/vii/index.shtm

FEMA Region VIII
(serving CO, MT, ND, SD, UT, WY)
Denver Federal Center
Building 710, Box 25267
Denver, CO 80255-0267
(303) 235-4800 FAX 303 235-4976
www.fema.gov/regions/viii/index.shtm

FEMA Region IX
(serving AZ, CA, HI, NV, TERRITORIES [i.e. AMERICAN SAMOA, GUAM, etc.])
1111 Broadway, Suite 1200
Oakland, CA 94607
(510) 627-7100 FAX 510 627-7112
www.fema.gov/regions/ix/index.shtm

FEMA Region X
(serving AK, ID, OR, WA)
Federal Regional Center
130 228th St., SW
Bothell, WA 98021-9796
(425) 487-4600 FAX 425 487-4622
www.fema.gov/regions/x/index.shtm

FEMA FOR KIDS:

FEMA has developed a fun web site for kids, so if you have access to the Internet, check out their information and games for kids of all ages:

http://www.fema.gov/kids/

FEMA PARTNERS:

Emergency management is not the result of one government agency alone. FEMA works with many government, non-profit and private sector agencies to assist the public in preparing for, responding to, and recovering from a disaster. Together, these players make up the emergency response "team."

- Local Emergency Management Agencies
- State Emergency Management Offices
- National Emergency Management Organizations
- Federal-level Partners
- Partnerships with the Private Sector

In addition to these partners, FEMA's Global Emergency Management System (GEMS) provides access to a wide variety of emergency management and disaster related web sites. *Please see FEMA's web site http://www.fema.gov for a complete listing of GEMS partners.*

DETAILED INFORMATION ABOUT FEMA PARTNERS:

• LOCAL EMERGENCY MANAGEMENT AGENCIES

Even the largest, most widespread disasters require a local response. So local emergency management programs are the heart of the nation's emergency management system. FEMA supports them with funding for emergency planning and equipment, by offering training courses for emergency managers and firefighters, by conducting exercises for localities to practice their response, and by promoting ways to minimize disasters' effects. FEMA also builds partnerships with mayors, county boards and other elected and appointed officials who share responsibility for emergency management.

• STATE EMERGENCY MANAGEMENT AGENCIES

Just like the local EMAs mentioned above, every state emergency management agency is an integral part of the emergency management system. State offices coordinate federal, state, and local resources for mitigation, preparedness, response and recovery operations.

STATE & TERRITORY EMERGENCY MANAGEMENT OFFICES

Alabama Emergency Management Agency
P.O. Drawer 2160
Clanton, AL 35046-2160
(205) 280-2200   FAX 205-280-2495
http://www.aema.state.al.us/

Alaska Division of Emergency Services
P.O. Box 5750
Fort Richardson, AK 99505-5750
(907) 428-7000 FAX 907 428-7009
http://www.ak-prepared.com/

American Samoa Territorial Emergency
Management Coordination (TEMCO)
American Samoa Government
P.O. Box 1086
Pago Pago, American Samoa 96799
(011)(684) 699-6415 FAX 011 684 699-6414

Arizona Division of Emergency Services
5636 East McDowell Road
Phoenix, AZ 85008
(602) 244-0504 FAX 602 231-6356
http://www.dem.state.az.us

Arkansas Dept of Emergency Management
P.O. Box 758
Conway, AR 72033
(501) 730-9750 FAX 501 730-9754
http://www.adem.state.ar.us/

California Governor's Office of Emergency
Services
P. O. Box 419047
Rancho Cordova, CA 95741-9047
(916) 845-8500 FAX 916 845-8444
http://www.oes.ca.gov/

Colorado Office of Emergency Management
Division of Local Government
Department of Local Affairs
15075 South Golden Road
Golden, CO 80401-3979
(303) 273-1622 FAX 303 273-1795
http://www.dola.state.co.us/oem/oemindex.htm

Connecticut Ofc of Emergency Management
Military Department
360 Broad Street
Hartford, CT 06105
(860) 566-3180 FAX 860 247-0664
http://www.mil.state.ct.us/oem.htm

Delaware Emergency Management Agency
165 Brick Store Landing Road
Smyrna, DE 19977
(302) 659-3362 FAX 302 659-6855
http://www.state.de.us/dema/

District of Columbia Emergency Management
Agency
2000 14th Street, NW, 8th Floor
Washington, DC 20009
(202) 727-6161 FAX 202 673-2290
http://dcema.dc.gov

Florida Division of Emergency Management
2555 Shumard Oak Blvd.
Tallahassee, FL 32399
(850) 413-9900 FAX 850 488-1016
http://www.floridadisaster.org

Georgia Emergency Management Agency
P.O. Box 18055
Atlanta, GA 30316-0055
(404) 635-7000 FAX 404 635-7205
http://www.state.ga.us/GEMA/

Guam Office of Civil Defense
P.O. Box 2877
Hagatna, Guam 96932
(011) (671) 475-9600 FAX 671 477-3727
http://ns.gov.gu/

Hawaii State Civil Defense
3949 Diamond Head Road
Honolulu, HI 96816-4495
(808) 734-4246 FAX 808 733-4287
http://www.scd.state.hi.us

Idaho Bureau of Disaster Services
Building 600
4040 Guard Street
Boise, ID 83705-5004
(208) 334-3460 FAX 208 334-2322
http://www.state.id.us/bds/

Illinois Emergency Management Agency
110 East Adams Street
Springfield, IL 62701
(217) 782-7860 FAX 217 782-2589
http://www.state.il.us/iema

Indiana Emergency Management Agency
Indiana Government Center South
Room E-208
302 W. Washington Street
Indianapolis, IN 46204
(317) 232-3980 FAX 317 232-3895
http://www.in.gov/sema/

Iowa Emergency Management Division
Level A
Hoover State Office Building
Des Moines, IA 50319
(515) 281-3231 FAX 515 281-7539
http://www.state.ia.us/government/dpd/emd/

Kansas Division of Emergency Management
2800 S.W. Topeka Boulevard
Topeka, KS 66611-1287
(785) 274-1409 FAX 785 274-1426
http://www.ink.org/public/kdem/

Kentucky Division of Emergency
Management
EOC Building
100 Minuteman Parkway
Frankfort, KY 40601-6168
(502) 607-1682 FAX 502 607-1614
http://kyem.dma.state.ky.us

Louisiana Office of Emergency Preparedness
7667 Independence Boulevard
Baton Rouge, LA 70804
(225) 925-7500 FAX 225 925-7501
http://www.loep.state.la.us

Maine Emergency Management Agency
State Office Building, Station 72
Augusta, ME 04333
(207) 626-4503 FAX 207 626-4499
http://www.state.me.us/mema/

Commonweath of the Northern **Mariana
Islands** Office of the Governor EMO
P. O. Box 10007
Saipan, Mariana Islands 96950
(670) 322-9529 FAX 670 322-9500
http://www.cnmiemo.org

National Disaster Management Office
Office of the Chief Secretary
P.O. Box 15
Majuro, Republic of **Marshall Islands** 96960
(011) (692) 625-5181 FAX 011 692 625-6896

Maryland Emergency Management Agency
Camp Fretterd Military Reservation
5401 Rue Saint Lo Drive
Reistertown, MD 21136
(410) 517-3600 FAX 410 517-3610
Tollfree 1-877-MEMA-USA
http://www.mema.state.md.us/

Massachusetts Emergency Management
Agency
400 Worcester Road
Framingham, MA 01702-5399
(508) 820-2000 FAX 508 820-2030
http://www.state.ma.us/mema/

Michigan Emergency Management Division
4000 Collins Road / P.O. Box 30636
Lansing, MI 48909-8136
(517) 333-5042 FAX 517 333-4987
http://www.msp.state.mi.us/division/emd/
emdweb1.htm

National Disaster Control Officer
Federated States of **Micronesia**
P.O. Box PS-53
Kolonia, Pohnpei - Micronesia 96941
(011) (691) 320-8815 FAX 011 691 320-2785

Minnesota Division of Emergency
Management
Emergency Response Commission
444 Cedar Street, Suite 223
St. Paul, MN 55101-6223
(651) 296-2233 FAX 651 296-0459
http://www.dem.state.mn.us

Mississippi Emergency Management Agency
P.O. Box 4501
Jackson, MS 39296-4501
(601) 352-9100 FAX 601 352-8314
Tollfree 1-800-442-MEMA (6362)
http://www.msema.org

Missouri Emergency Management Agency
2302 Militia Drive
Jefferson City, MO 65101
(573) 526-9100 FAX 573 634-7966
http://www.sema.state.mo.us/semapage.htm

Montana Disaster and Emergency Services
1900 Williams Street
P.O. Box 4789
Helena, MT 59604-4789
(406) 841-3911 FAX 406 841-3965
http://www.discoveringmontana.com/DMA/des

Nebraska Emergency Management Agency
1300 Military Road
Lincoln, NE 68508-1090
(402) 471-7430 FAX 402 471-7433
http://www.nebema.org

Nevada Division of Emergency Management
2525 South Carson Street
Carson City, NV 89701
(775) 687-4240 FAX 775 687-6788
http://www.dem.state.nv.us

New Hampshire Department of Public Safety
Div of Fire Safety & Emergency Management
Office of Emergency Management
10 Hazen Drive
Concord, NH 03305
(603) 271-2231 FAX 603 225-7341
http://www.nhoem.state.nh.us/

New Jersey Office of Emergency
Management
P.O. Box 7068
West Trenton, NJ 08628-0068
(609) 538-6050 FAX 609 538-0345
http://www.state.nj.us/njoem/

New Mexico Office of Emergency Services
and Security
Department of Public Safety
P.O. Box 1628
Santa Fe, NM 87504-1628
(505) 476-9600 FAX 505 476-9650
www.dps.nm.org/emergency/em_index.htm

New York State Emergency Management
Office
1220 Washington Avenue, Bldg # 22
Albany, NY 12226
(518) 457-2200 FAX 518 457-9995
http://www.nysemo.state.ny.us/

North Carolina Division of Emergency
Management
116 West Jones Street
Raleigh, NC 27603
(919) 733-3867 FAX 919 733-7554
http://www.dem.dcc.state.nc.us/

North Dakota Division of Emergency
Management
P.O. Box 5511
Bismarck, ND 58506-5511
(701) 328-8100 FAX 701 328-8181
http://www.state.nd.us/dem

Ohio Emergency Management Agency
2855 W. Dublin-Granville Road
Columbus, OH 43235-2206
(614) 889-7150 FAX 614 889-7183
http://www.state.oh.us/odps/division/ema/

Oklahoma Department of Civil Emergency
Management
P.O. Box 53365
Oklahoma City, OK 73152-3365
(405) 521-2481 FAX 405 521-4053
http://www.odcem.state.ok.us

Oregon Division of Emergency Management
595 Cottage Street, NE
Salem, OR 97310
(503) 378-2911 FAX 503 588-1378
http://www.osp.state.or.us/oem/index.htm

Palau NEMO Coordinator
Office of the President
P. O. Box 100
Koror, Republic of Paulau 96940
(011) (680) 488-2422 FAX 011 680 488-3312

Pennsylvania Emergency Management
Agency
P. O. Box 3321
Harrisburg, PA 17105-3321
(717) 651-2001 FAX 717 651-2040
http://www.pema.state.pa.us/

Puerto Rico Emergency Management Agency
P.O. Box 966597
San Juan, PR 00906-6597
(787) 724-0124 FAX 787 725-4244

Rhode Island Emergency Management Agcy
645 New London Ave
Cranston, RI 02920-3003
(401) 946-9996 Fax 401-944-1891
http://www.state.ri.us/riema/

South Carolina Emergency Management Div
1100 Fish Hatchery Road
West Columbia, SC 29172
(803) 737-8500 FAX 803 737-8570
http://www.scemd.org

South Dakota Div of Emergency Management
500 East Capitol
Pierre, SD 57501-5070
(605) 773-3231 FAX 605 773-3580
http://www.state.sd.us/military/sddem.htm

Tennessee Emergency Management Agency
3041 Sidco Drive
Nashville, TN 37204
(615) 741-0001 FAX 615 242-9635
http://www.tnema.org

Texas Department of Public Safety
Division of Emergency Management
P.O. Box 4087
Austin, TX 78773-0001
(512) 424-2138 FAX 512 424-2444
http://www.txdps.state.tx.us/dem/

Utah Division of Emergency Services and
Homeland Security
Room 1110, State Office Building
Salt Lake City, UT 84114
(801) 538-3400 FAX 801 338-3770
http://cem.utah.gov or http://des.utah.gov

Vermont Emergency Management
Waterbury State Complex
103 South Main Street
Waterbury, VT 05671-2101
(802) 244-8721 FAX 802 244-8655
http://www.dps.state.vt.us/vem/

Virgin Islands Territorial EM Agcy-VITEMA
2-C Contant, A-Q Building
St. Croix, VI 00820
(340) 774-2244 FAX 340 774-1491
http://www.usvi.org/vitema

Virginia Dept of Emergency Management
10501 Trade Court
Richmond, VA 23236-3713
(804) 897-6500 FAX 804 897-6626
http://www.vdem.state.va.us

Washington State Emergency Management Division
Building 20, M/S: TA-20
Camp Murray, WA 98430-5122
(253) 512-7000 FAX: 253 512-7200
http://www.wa.gov/wsem/

West Virginia Office of Emergency Services
Building 1, Room EB-80
1900 Kanawha Blvd. East
Charleston, WV 25305-0360
(304) 558-5380 FAX 304 344-4538
http://www.state.wv.us/wvoes/

Wisconsin Emergency Management
P.O. Box 7865
Madison, WI 53707-7865
(608) 242-3232 FAX 608 242-3247
http://badger.state.wi.us/agencies/dma/wem/index.htm

Wyoming Emergency Management Agency
5500 Bishop Blvd.
Cheyenne, WY 82009-3320
(307) 777-4900 FAX 307 635-6017
http://wema.state.wy.us

As of 31-Oct-2002 (per FEMA web site)
Fedhealth verified links as of 25-Nov-2002

• NATIONAL EMERGENCY MANAGEMENT ORGANIZATIONS

National Emergency Management Association (NEMA) - membership includes state emergency managers. **Internet:** http://www.nemaweb.org

International Association of Emergency Managers - membership includes local emergency managers. **Internet:** http://www.iaem.com

• FEMA's FEDERAL-LEVEL PARTNERS

Numerous federal agencies and departments are partners in the nation's emergency management system. Before a disaster, they participate in training exercises and activities to help the nation become prepared. During a catastrophic disaster, FEMA coordinates the federal response, working with 27 federal partners and the American Red Cross to provide emergency food and water, medical supplies and services, search and rescue operations, transportation assistance, environmental assessment, and more.

The National Disaster Medical System is a partnership set up to provide emergency medical services in a disaster, involving FEMA, the Department of Health and Human Services, the Department of Defense, the Veterans Administration, as well as public and private hospitals across the country.

• FEMA PARTNERSHIPS WITH THE PRIVATE SECTOR

FEMA encourages all sectors of society — from business and industry to volunteer organizations — to work together in disaster preparation, response and recovery. FEMA assists in coordinating activities of a variety of players, including private contractors, hospitals, volunteer organizations and area Businesses. It is through these partnerships of people working together that communities are able to put the pieces back together.

About the Canadian Red Cross:

Extracted from the Canadian Red Cross Disaster Services web site:

When disaster strikes in Canada or abroad, the quick response of Red Cross volunteers lessens the hardship suffered by victims. The Society provides personal disaster assistance to victims of emergencies, such as housefires. Through partnership agreements with federal, provincial and municipal governments, Red Cross also helps address the basic needs of Canadians affected by large-scale disasters.

The Red Cross helps people deal with situations that threaten their survival and safety; their security and well-being; and their human dignity -- in Canada and around the world.

All Red Cross assistance is provided free of charge, made possible by the generous contribution of people's time, money, and skills.

Contacting Your Local Canadian Red Cross:

There are a few different ways of finding your local Red Cross office:

If you have access to the Internet, you can check their national web site

http://www.redcross.ca

... or call ...

Canadian Red Cross
170 Metcalfe St., Suite 300
Ottawa, Ontario K2P 2P2
Phone: 613.740.1900 Fax: 613.740.1911

... or ...

Check your local telephone book in the white pages
for the Canadian Red Cross!

Write in your local office address & number here for future reference:

Your Local Canadian Red Cross Address:

_____

Telephone #: _____

About the Office of Critical Infrastructure Protection and Emergency Preparedness

Extracted from OCIPEP's web site www.ocipep.gc.ca as of April 2001:

As of February 2001, the **Office of Critical Infrastructure Protection and Emergency Preparedness (OCIPEP)** was created under the national leadership of the Minister of National Defence.

Canada's critical infrastructure -- includes key components of the energy and utilities, communications, services, transportation, safety and government sectors -- is increasingly dependent on information technology. This new organization will develop and implement a comprehensive approach to protecting this infrastructure.

OCIPEP is also the Government of Canada's primary agency for ensuring national civil emergency preparedness, encompassing the existing functions of Emergency Preparedness Canada.

How Canada's Emergency Preparedness System Works

First, it is up to the individual to know what to do in an emergency. If the individual is unable to cope, the different orders of government are expected to get involved and to respond, as their capabilities and resources are needed. Local emergency response organizations are normally first on the scene. If overwhelmed, they seek assistance from the province or territory, which, in turn, will ask the federal government for help if necessary.

To fulfill its mission, OCIPEP participates in a wide range of activities:

- Federal Civil Emergency Preparedness Planning
- Federal-Provincial-Territorial Cooperation
- International Cooperation
- Research
- Education and Training
- Emergency Operations
- Public Information
- SAFE GUARD

Federal Civil Emergency Preparedness Planning

OCIPEP, as the focal point for federal critical infrastructure preparedness and emergency preparedness activities, encourages the development of federal emergency planning, ensures the compatibility of plans among departments and agencies, and undertakes special projects or initiatives where national leadership is required.

FEDERAL-PROVINCIAL-TERRITORIAL COOPERATION

OCIPEP is the linchpin between the federal emergency preparedness community and those of provincial/territorial governments and - through them - municipalities. To support this function OCIPEP maintains a small regional office in each provincial capital.

OCIPEP administers the Joint Emergency Preparedness Program (JEPP), through which federal government, in consultation and cooperation with provincial and territorial governments, undertakes or contributes to projects that encourage a reasonably uniform emergency response capability across Canada. OCIPEP also administers the Disaster Financial Assistance Arrangements (DFAA) to assist provincial/territorial governments.

INTERNATIONAL COOPERATION

OCIPEP is responsible for coordinating international participation in the realm of civil emergency preparedness. OCIPEP coordinates and leads Canada's emergency preparedness activities in these areas, focusing primarily on NATO and the bilateral Canada/United States agreement.

RESEARCH

The Directorate, Research and Development (DRD) designs, coordinates and manages multidisciplinary studies undertaken in conjunction with other government departments and/or agencies outside government including universities, NGOs and private corporations which have an interest or responsibility in emergency preparedness. These studies contribute towards the advancement of knowledge in the fields of hazard assessment, disaster prediction, and mitigation of disasters. The Research and Development is also responsible for representing OCIPEP on national and international scientific committees and technical working groups.

EDUCATION AND TRAINING

OCIPEP provides emergency preparedness training to 1,600 participants yearly at the Canadian Emergency Preparedness College in Arnprior, Ontario. The College offers emergency planning and response courses to officials from federal departments, provincial/territorial and municipal governments, and private industry.

EMERGENCY OPERATIONS

Through the Government Emergency Operations Coordination Centre (GEOCC), OCIPEP maintains an around the clock monitoring and information centre of actual, potential and imminent disasters. GEOCC tracks indicators of emergencies and circulates advisory information on potential and actual emergencies that have implications for federal government and provincial authorities. The GEOCC is equipped and prepared to become the core of a federal emergency management system in the event the need arises.

PUBLIC INFORMATION

An important part of OCIPEP's emergency preparedness mandate is to ensure that Canadians are aware of the nature and possible impact of emergencies, the means of preventing or mitigating their effects, and the federal government's plans to respond. OCIPEP is also responsible for planning arrangements for coordinated public information during a national emergency, as defined by the Emergencies Act. OCIPEP provides a comprehensive program of public information related to a wide range of emergency preparedness activities and publishes the Emergency Preparedness Digest, a quarterly publication for those involved in emergency preparedness planning and management.

SAFE GUARD

Please see **APPENDIX B** after this section.

PROVINCIAL EMERGENCY MEASURES ORGANIZATIONS (EMOS)

Headquarters
Office of Critical Infrastructure Protection and Emergency Preparedness (OCIPEP)
122 Bank Street
Jackson Building, 2nd Floor
Ottawa, ON K1A 0W6
Tel: (613) 991-7035 Fax: (613) 998-9589
Communications@ocipep-bpiepc.gc.ca
http://www.ocipep-bpiepc.gc.ca

Newfoundland and Labrador
Emergency Measures Organization
Department of Municipal & Provincial Affairs
P.O. Box 8700
St. John's, NF A1B 4J6
Tel: (709) 729-3703 Fax: (709) 729-3857
http://www.gov.nf.ca/mpa/emo.html

Prince Edward Island
Emergency Measures Organization
134 Kent Street
Charlottetown, PE   C1A 8R8
Tel: (902) 368-6361 Fax: (902) 368-6362
http://www.gov.pe.ca/commcul/emo/

Nova Scotia
Nova Scotia Emergency Measures Organization
P.O. Box 2581
Halifax, NS   B3J 3N5
Tel: (902) 424-5620 Fax: (902) 424-5376
http://www.gov.ns.ca/emo/

New Brunswick
New Brunswick Emergency Measures Organization
Department of Public Safety
P.O. Box 6000
Fredericton, NB   E3B 5H1
Tel: (506) 453-2133 Fax: (506) 453-5513
http://www.gnb.ca/cnb/emo-omu/index-e.htm

Québec
Direction générale de la Sécurité civile
Ministry of Public Security/Ministère de la Securité publique
2525, boul. Laurier, 5e étage
Sainte-Foy, QC G1V 2L2
Tel: (418) 644-6826 Fax: (418) 643-3194
http://www.msp.gouv.qc.ca

Ontario
Emergency Measures Ontario
Ministry of Public Safety and Security
77 Wellesley St. West
Box 222
Toronto, ON M7A 1N3
Tel: (416) 314-3723 Fax: (416) 314-3758
http://www.sgcs.gov.on.ca/english/public/
emo.html

Manitoba
Manitoba Emergency Management
Organization (MEMO)
405 Broadway Avenue, Room 1525
Winnipeg, MB R3C 3L6
Tel: (204) 945-4772 Fax: (204) 945-4620
Tollfree 1-888-267-8298
http://www.gov.mb.ca/gs/memo/index.html

Saskatchewan
Saskatchewan Emergency Planning
220-1855 Victoria Avenue
Regina, SK S4P 3V7
Tel: (306) 787-9563 Fax: (306) 787-1694
www.municipal.gov.sk.ca/safety/SEP.shtml

Alberta
Disaster Services Branch
Alberta Municipal Affairs
16th Floor, Commerce Place
10155-102nd Street
Edmonton, AB T5J 4L4
Tel: (780) 422-9000 Fax: (780) 422-1549
http://www.gov.ab.ca/ma/ds/

British Columbia
Provincial Emergency Program Headquarters
P.O. Box 9201 Station Prov. Govt.
Victoria, BC V8W 9J1
Tel: (250) 952-4913 Fax: (250) 952-4888
http://www.pep.bc.ca

PEP Vancouver Island Region
455 Boleskine Road
Victoria, BC V8Z 1E7
(250) 952-5848 Fax: (250) 952-4983

PEP South West Region
9800- 140th Street
Surrey, BC V3T 4M5
(604) 586-2665 Fax: (604) 586-4334

PEP South East Region
403 Vernon Street
Nelson, BC V1L 4E6
(250) 354-6395 Fax: (250) 354-6561

PEP Central Region
1255-D Dalhousie Drive
Kamloops, BC V2C 5Z5
(250) 371-5240 Fax: (250) 371-5246

PEP North East Region
1541 South Ogilvie Street
Prince George, BC V2N 1W7
(250) 612-4172 Fax: (250) 612-4171

PEP North West Region
2914 Eby Street
Terrace, BC V8G 2X5
(250) 638-2151 Fax: (250) 638-2152

Northwest Territories
Emergency Measures Organization
Dept. of Municipal and Community Affairs
Government of Northwest Territories
600, 5201-50th Avenue - Northwest Tower
Yellowknife, NT X1A 3S9
Tel: (867) 873-7083 or 873-7785
Fax: (867) 873-8193
www.maca.gov.nt.ca/about/emergency.html

Yukon
Emergency Measures Branch
Community Services
Government of Yukon
P.O. Box 2703
Whitehorse, YK Y1A 2C6
Tel: (867) 667-5220 Fax: (867) 393-6266
http://www.gov.yk.ca/depts/community/emo/

Nunavut
Nunavut Emergency Services
Department of Community Government and
Transportation
P. O. Box 1000, Station 700
Iqaluit, NU X0A 0H0
Tel: (867) 975-5300 Fax: (867) 979-4221

Per OCIPEP's site www.ocipep-bciepc.gc.ca
and www.emergencypreparednessweek.ca site

Fedhealth verified info & links: 2002-04-30

FOR HELP OUTSIDE
CANADA & THE UNITED STATES

The following was extracted from the IFRC web site as of November 2000:

The **International Federation of Red Cross and Red Crescent Societies** is the world's largest humanitarian organization providing assistance without discrimination as to nationality, race, religious beliefs, class or political opinions.

Founded in 1919, the International Federation comprises 176 member Red Cross and Red Crescent societies, a Secretariat in Geneva and more than 60 delegations strategically located to support activities around the world. There are more societies in formation. The Red Crescent is used in place of the Red Cross in many Islamic countries.

The Federation's mission is to improve the lives of vulnerable people by mobilizing the power of humanity. Vulnerable people are those who are at greatest risk from situations that threaten their survival, or their capacity to live with an acceptable level of social and economic security and human dignity. Often, these are victims of natural disasters, poverty brought about by socio-economic crises, refugees, and victims of health emergencies.

The Federation's work focuses on four core areas: promoting humanitarian values, disaster response, disaster preparedness, and health and community care. For more information, please visit IFRC on the Internet or contact:

INTERNATIONAL FEDERATION OF RED CROSS AND RED CRESCENT SOCIETIES

P. O. Box 372   Phone: (+41 22) 730 42 22
CH-1211 Geneva 19   Fax: (+41 22) 733 03 95
Switzerland   Telex: 412 133 FRC CH

Internet: http://www.ifrc.org

E-Mail: secretariat@ifrc.org

Or find your local National Society via the **Directory** link on the Internet. *(The online Directory has an alphabetic listing by country of all the Red Cross and Red Crescent Societies worldwide.)*

APPENDIX A

Office of Homeland Security, Office of National Preparedness and Citizen Corps

What is the Office of Homeland Security (OHS)?

The President's Executive Order established the Office of Homeland Security and the Homeland Security Council to develop and coordinate a comprehensive national strategy to strengthen protections against terrorist threats or attacks in the United States. The new team coordinates federal, state, and local counter-terrorism efforts to detect, prepare for, prevent, protect against, respond to, and recover from terrorist attacks within the U.S.

What is the Homeland Security Advisory System (HSAS)?

The Homeland Security Advisory System provides a comprehensive and effective means to disseminate information regarding the risk of terrorist acts to Federal, State, and local authorities and to the American people. This system provides warnings in the form of a set of graduated color-coded "Threat Conditions" that increase as the risk of the threat increases.

HSAS's "Threat Conditions" or "Threat Levels":

SEVERE = **RED** (Severe risk of terrorist attacks)

HIGH – **ORANGE** (High risk of terrorist attacks)

ELEVATED = **YELLOW** (Significant risk of terrorist attacks)

GUARDED = **BLUE** (General risk of terrorist attacks)

LOW = **GREEN** (Low risk of terrorist attacks)

Alerts and threat conditions can be declared for the entire nation, or for a specific geographic area, functional or industrial sector. The general public should stay current with news and alerts issued through the media.

Office of Homeland Security web site: www.whitehouse.gov/homeland/

What is the Office of National Preparedness?

In May 2001 FEMA created the Office of National Preparedness (ONP) to coordinate all federal programs between the various agencies dealing with chemical, biological, radiological, or nuclear weapons consequence management. Many of these programs offer training, planning and assistance to state and local governments but there was no single point of contact in the federal government for emergency responders, state and local officials.

The Office of National Preparedness is now the central coordination point working very closely with many federal, state and local agencies and departments including the Office of Homeland Security.

What is the mission of the Office of National Preparedness?

The mission and overriding objective of the ONP at FEMA is to help this country be prepared to respond to acts of terrorism.

ONP's three main focuses:

- **First Responder Initiative** - Provide the support that local responders (firefighters, police officers, emergency medical teams, etc.) need to do their jobs and work together effectively. Some examples include improving access to funds for developing plans, acquiring equipment and training, and setting national standards for compatible equipment to communicate efficiently.

- **Central Point of Contact for Federal Terrorism Preparedness Programs** - First responders need a single point of contact within the federal government to help them respond to terrorist events. Since FEMA already has over 20 years of experience coordinating up to 26 agencies ONP was a natural fit.

- **Citizen Corps** - A broad network of volunteer efforts of citizens to prepare local communities to effectively prevent and respond to the threats of terrorism, crime, or any kind of disaster. Citizen Corps efforts at state and local levels will be coordinated nationally by the Federal Emergency Management Agency (FEMA).

Some groups participating in Citizen Corps include...

Citizen Corps Councils
Community Emergency Response Teams (CERTs)
Neighborhood Watch Program (NWP)
Volunteers in Police Service (VIPS)

To learn more about **Citizen Corps** visit www.citizencorps.gov

APPENDIX B

SAFE GUARD / SAUVE GARDE
Emergency Preparedness Partners in Canada
Les partenaires de la protection civile au Canada

What is SAFE GUARD?

SAFE GUARD is a national public information program aimed at increasing public awareness of emergency preparedness in Canada.

Through this program, government, private and voluntary organizations - part of the emergency planning, response and recovery community - are invited to identify themselves as SAFE GUARD partners in carrying out their communications and public awareness activities.

As a public recognition focus for the emergency preparedness community, the SAFE GUARD label visually highlights common goals and objectives and promotes co-operation among partner organizations.

How does it work?

As a member of SAFE GUARD network, partner organizations are invited to use the SAFE GUARD label on public information materials related to their emergency preparedness programs or activities.

A common symbol used by various organizations will demonstrate the broad interest in emergency preparedness, create links among various organizations and encourage partnership.

Who are the SAFE GUARD partners?

Organizations with a defined role or interest in ensuring and promoting the safety and security of Canadians in the face of actual and potential emergencies:

- Governments: federal, provincial/territorial and local
- Non-governmental organizations
- Volunteer organizations
- Training and educational organizations
- Business and industry
- Professional associations

Key benefits of SAFE GUARD

* No cost for membership. SAFE GUARD is a national network that serves as a focus for sharing and developing communications activities, and as a window to distribute your emergency preparedness messages through partnership initiatives. It can help you maximize the impact of your messages and enhance your corporate or institutional links.

* Shared expertise and increased efficiency. In times of dwindling resources SAFE GUARD gives partners the opportunity to combine their resources, save time, and reduce costs.

* Access to leading-edge information technologies such as the Internet. As a partner, you may put your emergency preparedness information on the SAFE GUARD NET or establish a link between your own site and the SAFE GUARD site. SAFE GUARD NET is intended to become the main Canadian Internet depository of publicly available information on emergency preparedness.

* Use the SAFE GUARD label on public information/education products. This is a tangible way to demonstrate you belong to the Canadian emergency preparedness community and share common goals.

* Opportunity to participate in joint communications initiatives with a variety of national governmental, non-governmental and private sector organizations that share a similar interest in and concern for emergency preparedness.

* Free subscription to the SAFE GUARD newsletter; members are invited to use it as an information exchange.

How can you become a SAFE GUARD partner?

Interested organizations are invited to contact the SAFE GUARD Secretariat to obtain the program guidelines. Through the SAFE GUARD Secretariat, organizations can also learn about and be put in touch with other partners.

Safeguard Secretariat
122 Bank St., 2nd Floor
Ottawa, ON K1A 0W6
Phone: 1-800-830-3118
Fax: (613) 998-9589
E-mail: safeguard@epc-pcc.gc.ca
Internet: www.safeguard.ca

APPENDIX C

*The following **SAMPLE GUIDELINE / DATABASE** was developed by South Carolina's Charleston County Emergency Preparedness Department. A list of acronyms used in the following 6 pages is included on page 179.*

Any County Emergency Preparedness
Terrorism Emergency Operations Outline

Counteractions Standard Operations Guide

I. GENERAL

A. *Purpose*

The purpose of this SOG is to assist other officials and emergency service personnel with a working outline for developing a written set of guidelines for the conduct of antiterrorism and terrorism counteraction response operations. Contact your local emergency management agency for assistance.

This outline of antiterrorism is designed to deter and limit the success of terrorists acts against government / industry resources / personnel and facilities while Counteraction facilitates response to, and recovery from, an actual terrorist incident. The collection and dissemination of timely threat intelligence information, informative public awareness programs, and through the implementation of sound defensive mitigation measures usually insure the best countermeasures one may accomplish.

B. *Authority*

The listing of any local city, county, state or federal ordinances as may be applicable for the intended jurisdictions being protected.

C. *References*
1. Presidential Decision Directive 39 [PDD-39], June 1995.
2. State Terrorism Incident Annexes.

3. Local Community Bomb Threat Incident Plan.

4. Emergency Response To Incidents Involving Chemical And Biological Warfare Agents.

5. Terrorism In The U.S. 1982-1992, FBI Report.

6. The Federal Response Plan [FRP], Terrorism Annex.

7. Local Airport, Seaport, Transportation, Dam, or Utilities Emergency Counter Terrorism Plan.

8. Emergency Response to Terrorism Job Aid, May 2000.

9. II CT Chemical / Biological Incident Handbook.

D. *Definitions*

A list as detailed or as brief as may be applicable to the depth of your SOG. Contact your local emergency management agency for assistance.

E. *Organizations*

Apply a basic organization chart for primary agencies that may be anticipated to support the various aspects of your SOG. Federal, state, city / county and local. See the local emergency management agency plan.

II. SITUATION

A. *International Terrorism*

International terrorism continues as a threat and although it has been primarily rooted in other countries, a great number of Americans have been affected by these acts. According to the U.S. Department of State and as reported in the media large numbers of the actual terrorist attacks worldwide were targeted against Americans. The impact of international terrorism still has vivid images occurring almost worldwide.

B. *Domestic Terrorism*

Statistics provided by the FBI prior to the mid-1980's indicated only a few acts of terrorism inside the United States as influenced by international terrorism. Since the 1993 bombing of the World Trade Center in New York it was a clear reminder that the United States is not immune from acts of international terrorism based within our borders.

It is very clear that managing the consequences of terrorism in this country from any source can be a most difficult and challenging task. Trying to recover from such senseless terrorist events has already begun to change the way Americans view the potential threats and mass effect from a single terrorist act perpetrated in local communities.

C. *Conditions*

1. Actual events or threat of a terrorist act may cause implementation of precautionary measures from as high up as Presidential sources.

2. The FBI will likely implement a crisis management law enforcement response to any significant threat or actual act of terrorism and include threat assessment / consultation and NBC / WMD Technical Assistance.

3. Incidents that occur without advance threat or warning and that produce major consequences. FEMA will probably respond and implement within the FRP consequence managment activities.

D. *Planning Assumptions*

No single agency at any government level has the unilateral authority or all the knowledge and skills to act in a terrorist event, especially WMD / WME. The SOG will be activated upon such threat or an actual event.

Certain instances will require, as in NBC events, that perimeters be set and closed to authorized officials and first responders as well. The SOG may also have to request activation of specialty service resources and/or task forces. Your local emergency management plans may assist this step.

III. CONCEPT OF OPERATIONS

A. *Crisis Management*

1. Local Law Enforcement generally has the lead responsibility

for implementing SOG crisis management.

2. Each participating agency will maintain a current copy of the Terrorism Response Alert List of the SOG.

3. A systematic scene approach will often be implemented while self-protective measures as appropriate are taken towards controlling the situation. The IMS / ICS framework and possible transition into the Unified Command System may be used as soon as possible.

4. Responders SITREP, staging, direction and command & control information all within often dynamic incident events as agencies / personnel and equipment arrive in force.

5. Communications size-up will be CONTINUOUS in such a dynamic incident and should address scene stability in the SOG (e.g. stable, deteriorated, continuing to deterioriate, unsafe).

6. To avoid infrastructure gridlock, establish from the initial SITREP the priorities needed for life safety and protection. Address immediate and sequential response structuring.

B. *Consequence Management*

This level of management integrates all aspects of the response that will generally protect the public's health and safety, manage fears and suffering, and enhance evidence-gathering towards identifying and eventually apprehending the perpetrators. For assistance contact your local emergency management agency.

1. Pre-Incident Phase

   a. Protective actions such as organizational SOG's aimed at coordinating any threat in the local area via an identified part of a Command Group. Threatcon Alpha or Bravo.

   b. SOG's that establish actions and security awareness measures that prepare a counter deterrence to terrorist vulnerabilities.

2. Trans-Incident Phase

   a. This phase involves the threat emerging to an actual act or imminent action of terrorism. Threatcon Charlie.

   b. Everyone should stay focused on the end objective to

"save lives" and coordinate cooperative agencies' efforts to solve most disagreements. ROC's, JOC's, JIC's, EOC's, IST's, IAP's, SOG.

3. Post-Incident Phase

   a. This phase may involve an incident that occurred without any advance warning and produces major consequences and appears to be an act of terrorism. Many concurrent efforts of crisis management will be initiated to establish a short term Incident Action Plan.

   b. Local officials will mitigate the situation to the best of their ability until further supported by the combined state and federal resources tasked.

4. Disengagement

   a. If no act of terrorism occurs then the federal response will disengage as coordinated. Stand down will occur for all according to their SOP's / SOG's.

   b. All agencies that responded will be requested to turn in a copy of their incident logs, journals, messages, or other non-sensitive records to the local coordinating agency. This information will be key to establishing an accurate post incident critique. Critiques are often delayed pending any legal requirements to keep certain information in confidence.

   c. PISD (post incident stress debriefings) will be offered by the proper mental health agency for responders based on the nature of the event and it's circumstances.

IV. RESPONSIBILITIES

A. *Crisis and Consequence Management*

   1. The County Sheriff LNO will: develop local SOG's.

   2. Local Response Agencies will: develop local SOG's.

B. *EOC - JOC Support Agencies*

Agencies not covered in this SOG are understood for mutual aid response to assist neighboring communities. See attached map.

(Suggestion: Include a map with your plan indicating areas being covered by Support Agencies.)

V. LOCAL STATE FEDERAL INTERFACE

This SOG is supported by the Terrorism Incident Annex to the Federal Response Plan and your State Emergency Operations Plan to include any Regional Task Force operational concepts applicable. Contact your local Emergency Management Agency for assistance in available plans.

VI. PRIMARY POINT OF CONTACT

Inquiries or changes concerning this SOG Outline should be addressed to Charleston County EPD, Project Officer for Terrorism Incident Management, 4045 Bridge View Drive, North Charleston, S.C. 29405-7464 or 843-202-7400 and Fax 843-202-7408.

DISCLAIMER: Information provided is solely intended as a sample guideline / database and neither the County of Charleston nor any agency, officer or employee warrants the accuracy, reliability or timeliness of any information in the Terrorism Counteraction SOG database. While every effort is made to ensure a broad accuracy of this information, portions may be incorrect or not current for all circumstances and we shall not be liable for any losses caused by such reliance on this outline information. Any persons or entities who relies on information obtained from this database does so at his or her own risk.

Acronyms

Used in the preceding "County Emergency Preparedness Terrorism Emergency Operations Outline"

B-NICE - Biological, Nuclear Incendiary, Chemical
        or Explosive Device

CAT - Crisis Action Team

CBR - Chemical, Biological, Radiological

EOC - Emergency Operations Center

EPD - Emergency Preparedness Division

FEMA - Federal Emergency Management Agency

FRP - Federal Response Plan

IAP - Incident Action Plan

ICS - Incident Command System

IMS - Incident Management System

IST - Incident Support Team

JIC - Joint Incident Command

JOC - Joint Operations Center

LNO - LIAISON Officer

NBC - Nuclear, Biological, Chemical devices

PISD - Post Incident Stress Debriefings

ROC - Regional Operations Center

SITREP - Situation Report

SOP - Standard Operating Procedures

SOG - Standard Operating Guidelines

Threatcon - Terrorist Threat Condition

WME - Weapons of Mass Effect

WMD - Weapons of Mass Destruction

END NOTES

[1] United States Department of Commerce National Oceanic and Atmospheric Administration, "Answers to La Niña Frequently Asked Questions", "Why do El Niño and La Niña occur?", (www.elnino.noaa.gov/lanina_new_faq.html), 1999.

[2] United States Environmental Protection Agency, "Global Warming: Climate - An Introduction", (www.epa.gov/globalwarming/climate/index.html), 2001.

[3] Patricia Reaney, "Increase in Greenhouse Gases Seen From Space" (Reuters online, March 14, 2001).

RESOURCES

Abramovitz, Janet N., "Natural disasters – At the hand of God or man?", Environmental News Network (ENN) Features, 23 June 1999, Copyright 1999, Worldwatch Institute.

Accidental First Aid Training®. *First Aid Made Easy*, New South Wales, Australia: Accidental First Aid Supplies Pty Ltd, 1995.

American Heart Association. *Guidelines 2000 for Cardiopulmonary Resuscitation and Emergency Cardiovascular Care, International Consensus on Science*, Volume 11, Number 3, Fall 2000.

American Red Cross. *Are You Ready for a Heat Wave?* Washington, D.C.: The American National Red Cross, 1998.

American Red Cross. *Are You Ready for a Thunderstorm?* Washington, D.C.: The American National Red Cross, 1998.

American Red Cross. *Coping With Disaster – Emotional Health Issues for Victims*, Washington, D.C.: The American National Red Cross, 1991.

American Red Cross. *Disaster Preparedness for Seniors by Seniors,* Washington, D.C.: The American National Red Cross and the Rochester-Monroe County Chapter of the American Red Cross, 1995.

American Red Cross. *Family Disaster Plan and Personal Survival Guide*, Washington, D.C.: The American National Red Cross, 1989.

American Red Cross. *First Aid Fast*, Washington, D.C.:The American National Red Cross, 1995.

American Red Cross and California Community Foundation. *Disaster Preparedness for Disabled & Elderly People,* Washington, D.C.: The American National Red Cross, 1985.

American Red Cross Los Angeles Chapter, *The Emergency Survival Handbook,* Los Angeles, CA: Los Angeles Chapter, American Red Cross, 1985.

American Red Cross Los Angeles Chapter – Third Edition, *Safety and Survival in an Earthquake,* Los Angeles, CA: L. A. Chapter, American Red Cross, 1986.

De Blij, H. J., *Nature on the Rampage,* Smithsonian Institute, Washington D.C.: Smithsonian Books, 1994.

Editors of BACKPACKER® Magazine, *All Weather All Season Trip Planner,* Emmaus, PA:Rodale Press, Inc., 1997.

Emergency Preparedness Canada, *Disaster Financial Assistance Arrangements (DFAA),* (http://www.epc-pcc.ca/) Public Information / Resources, Ontario, 2000.

Emergency Preparedness Canada, British Columbia Provincial Emergency Program, Canadian Mortgage and Housing Corporation, Health Canada, Geological Survey of Canada, Insurance Bureau of Canada, *Earthquakes in Canada?,* Her Majesty the Queen in Right of Canada, Department of Natural Resources Canada, 1996.

Emergency Preparedness Canada, Canadian Geographic, Environment Canada, Geological Survey of Canada, Insurance Bureau of Canada, Natural Resources Canada, Statistics Canada, The Weather network, *Natural Hazards - a National Atlas of Canada,* Canadian Services Canada, 1997.

Emergency Preparedness Canada, Safe Guard, and Environment Canada, *Severe Storms,* Minister of Supply and Services Canada, 1997.

Federal Emergency Management Agency, *Are You Ready? Your Guide to Disaster Preparedness,*Washington, D.C., 1993.

Federal Emergency Management Agency, *Extreme Heat Fact Sheet & Backgrounder*, Washington, D.C., 1998.

Federal Emergency Management Agency, *Facts About Flood Insurance,* Washington, D.C., 1996.

Federal Emergency Management Agency, *Good Ideas Book – How People and Communities Are Preparing For Disaster*, Washington, D.C., 1993.

Federal Emergency Management Agency, *Hazardous Materials Fact Sheet & Backgrounder*, Washington, D.C., 1998.

Federal Emergency Management Agency, *The Humane Society of the United States Offers Disaster Planning Tips for Pets, Livestock and Wildlife*, Washington, D.C., 1997.

Federal Emergency Management Agency, *Landslides and Mudflows Fact Sheet & Backgrounder*, Washington, D.C., 1998.

Federal Emergency Management Agency, *National Flood Insurance Coverage Available to Homeowners*, Washington, D.C., 1996.

Federal Emergency Management Agency, *Nuclear Power Plant Emergency Fact Sheet & Backgrounder*, Washington, D.C., 1997.

Federal Emergency Management Agency, *Project Impact: Building a Disaster Resistant Community,* Washington, D.C., 1998.

Federal Emergency Management Agency, *Returning Home After the Disaster – An Information Pamphlet for FEMA Disaster Workers*, Washington, D.C., 1987.

Federal Emergency Management Agency, *Terrorism Fact Sheet & Backgrounder*, Washington, D.C., 1998.

Federal Emergency Management Agency, *Volcanoes Fact Sheet & Backgrounder*, Washington, D.C., 1998.

Federal Emergency Management Agency and the American Red Cross, *Disaster Preparedness Coloring Book*, Washington D.C., 1993.

Federal Emergency Management Agency and the American Red Cross, *Emergency Preparedness Checklist*, Washington D.C., 1993.

Federal Emergency Management Agency and the American Red Cross, *Food and Water in an Emergency*, Washington D.C., 1994.

Federal Emergency Management Agency and the American Red Cross, *Helping Children Cope with Disaster*, Washington D.C., 1993.

Federal Emergency Management Agency and the American Red Cross, *Preparing for Emergencies - A Checklist for People with Mobility Problems*, Washington D.C., 1995.

Federal Emergency Management Agency and the American Red Cross, *Your Family Disaster Plan,* Washington D.C., 1991.

Federal Emergency Management Agency and the American Red Cross, *Your Family Disaster Supplies Kit,* Washington D.C., 1992.

Federal Emergency Management Agency, the American Red Cross, The Home Depot, National Association of Home Builders, Georgia Emergency Management Agency, *Against the Wind - Protecting Your Home from Hurricane Wind Damage,* Washington D.C., 1993.

Federal Emergency Management Agency and the United States Fire Administration, *Wildfire: Are You Prepared?* Washington D.C., 1993.

Federal Emergency Management Agency and the Wind Engineering Research Center at Texas Tech University, *Taking Shelter From the Storm Building a Safe Room Inside Your House, Second Edition,* Washington D.C., August 1999.

Information on avalanches obtained from the Internet online information page, "Avalanche Awareness", (http://www-nsidc.colorado.edu/NSIDC/EDUCATION/AVALANCHE/) maintained by the National Snow and Ice Data Center, University of Colorado, Boulder, November 2000.

Mark Mayell and the Editors of *Natural Health* Magazine, *The Natural Health First-Aid Guide: the definitive handbook of natural remedies for treating minor emergencies*, New York: Pocket Books, 1994.

Microsoft Corporation. "Earthquake," Microsoft® Encarta® Online Encyclopedia 2001 http://encarta.msn.com © 1997-2001.

Microsoft Corporation. "Meteorology," Microsoft® Encarta® Online Encyclopedia 2001 http://encarta.msn.com © 1997-2001.

Reader's Digest, *Natural Disasters (The Earth, Its Wonders, Its Secrets)*, London, The Reader's Digest Association, Limited, 1996.

State of California Department of Conservation and National landslide information Center, U.S. Geological Survey, "Features That May Indicate Catastrophic Landslide Movement", Denver, November 1998.

Survivor Industries, Inc., The Wallace Guidebook for Emergency Care and Survival", Newbury Park, CA: H. Wallace, 1989.

Swift Aid USA, *Swift+Aid to First Aid "What To Do In An Emergency"*, Toledo, Ohio, 1990

United Nations Environment Programme, "Global Warming Report Details Impacts On People and Nature", Bonn/Geneva/Nairobi, 19Feb2001.

U.S.D.A. Forest Service National Avalanche Center, "Avalanche Basics": (http://www.avalanche.org/~nac/), November 2000.

ADDITIONAL RESOURCES & WEB SITES

AMERICAN RED CROSS DISASTER SERVICES:

After Disaster Strikes – How to recover *financially* from a natural disaster
The American Red Cross, the Federal Emergency Management Agency, and the
National Endowment for Financial Education published the original brochure.
http://www.redcross.org/disaster/safety/after.html

Talking About Disaster: Guide for Standard Messages
This online information developed by The National Disaster Education Coalition
was reviewed to ensure accuracy of information used in this Manual. Members of
the National Disaster Education Coalition include the American Red Cross,
FEMA, NOAA/National Weather Service, National Fire Protection Association,
U.S. Geological Survey, Institute for Business and Home Safety, International
Association of Emergency Managers, U.S. Dept. of Agriculture Cooperative State
Research, Education, and Extension Service.

The Guide is a set of standard disaster safety messages on many hazards as well as
general disaster safety information and is viewable through web pages or using
downloadable PDF files. http://www.redcross.org/disaster/safety/guide.html

FEDERAL EMERGENCY MANAGEMENT AGENCY (FEMA):

FEMA for Kids   http://www.fema.gov/kids/

FEMA Library   http://www.fema.gov/library/
From the LEGAL Room - Congressional Testimony section:
STATEMENT OF BRUCE BAUGHMAN, FEMA'S Director for the Office of
National Preparedness' to Committee on Transportation and Infrastructure
Subcommittee on Economic Development, Public Buildings, and Emergency
Management - U.S. House of Representatives, 04/11/02.

FEMA Federal Insurance & Mitigation Administration http://www.fema.gov/fima

FEMA Preparedness, Training & Exercises http://www.fema.gov/pte
Searched in the SPEECHES section:
REMARKS BY KAY C. GOSS, CEM® FEMA'S Associate Director for
Preparedness, Training, and Exercises "General Session: Disaster Preparedness,
Mitigation, and Sustainability", Coronado Springs Hotel, Orlando, FL, 4/27/98.

FEMA Response & Recovery http://www.fema.gov/r-n-r/
HOW CAN I... WHERE CAN I... WHAT IF...*(Frequently Asked Questions)*

To order materials produced by FEMA contact your local or state EM office *(see
Section 4)*. Or link to the FEMA web site: http://www.fema.gov
Or call FEMA: 1-800-480-2520 M-F 8a-5p Eastern, Fax (301) 497-6378, or write
to: FEMA, P.O. Box 2012, Jessup, MD 20794-2012

OFFICE OF CRITICAL INFRASTRUCTURE PROTECTION AND EMERGENCY PREPAREDNESS (OCIPEP): http://www.ocipep.gc.ca
(Public Information/Resources, Research Information, Safeguard, Who We Are)

MISCELLANEOUS SITES:

Allstate Insurance Company's Resources and Tools - National Catastrophe Team Tips: http://www.allstate.com/catastrophe/

American Avalanche Association's Information/Media and Education links: http://www.avalanche.org/~aaap/

American Family Insurance's Safety & Loss Control links: http://www.amfam.com

Canada Mortgage and Housing Corporation's Online Publications http://www.cmhc.ca

Canadian Avalanche Association, Avalanche Courses, Avalanche Safety Training: http://www.avalanche.ca

Canadian Centre for Emergency Preparedness http://www.ccep.ca

Canadian Red Cross http://www.redcross.ca

Disaster Recovery Information Exchange (DRIE) Canada http://www.drie.org

Emergency Response & Research Institute's EmergencyNettm http://emergency.com

Environment Canada http://www.ec.gc.ca

Heart and Stroke Foundation of Canada, Health Matters, Resource Library: http://www.na.heartandstroke.ca

Institute for Business and Home Safety http://www.ibhs.org

Institute for Catastrophic Loss Reduction, Toronto, Ontario, Canada: http://www.iclr.org

Insurance Bureau of Canada, Home Insurance, News Media, and Publications: http://www.ibc.ca

Integrated Forest Fire Management Project (IFFM): http://www.iffm.or.id

Manti-LaSal Avalanche Center, USFS Utah Avalanche Center: http://www.avalanche.org/~lsafc/

Munich Reinsurance Company's Press Releases: http://www.munichre.com

National Fire Data Center: http://www.usfa.fema.gov

National Interagency Fire Center, Boise, Idaho: http://www.nifc.gov

National Oceanic and Atmospheric Administration (NOAA)
Atlantic Oceanographic & Meteorological Laboratory http://www.aoml.noaa.gov
National Climatic Data Center http://www.ncdc.noaa.gov/ol/ncdc.html
NOAA Office of Public Affairs National Weather Service
Natural Disaster Reduction Initiative http://www.nws.noaa.gov/pa/

Natural Resources Canada: http://www.nrcan.gc.ca

Pacific Tsunami Warning Center (Hawaii): http://www.nws.noaa.gov/pr/ptwc

PBS Online's SAVAGE EARTH: http://www.pbs.org/wnet/savageearth/

SAFE GUARD Emergency Preparedness Partners in Canada's Publications:
http://www.safeguard.ca

State Farm Insurance's Life Events Tips: http://www.statefarm.com

Statistics Canada http://www.statcan.ca

The Hartford Homeowners Insurance Home Safety Tips: http://thehartford.com

United Nations Environment Programme http://www.unep.org

University of Washington Department of Geophysics' WWW server
TOPIC under General Tsunami Information: Tsunami Hazard Mitigation
(originally developed by Benjamin Cook, 1995)
http://www.geophys.washington.edu/tsunami/intro.html

U.S.D.A. Forest Service National Avalanche Center
http://www.avalanche.org/~nac/

U.S. Department of Defense DefenseLINK News & Publications:
http://www.defenselink.mil

U.S. Nuclear Regulatory Commission http://www.nrc.gov

Volcano World http://volcano.und.nodak.edu/vw.html

West Coast / Alaska Tsunami Warning Center http://wcatwc.gov

INDEX

A

9-1-1, tips for calling, 24
activated charcoal, uses for, 27, 68
air pollution, ozone alerts, 105
ambulance, tips for calling, 24
American Red Cross. *See also* Canadian Red Cross
   assistance programs following disasters, 150-152
   contact information, 156
   safety programs, 20
   Web site, 21, 184
ammonia, pain relief uses for, 31
avalanches. *See also* landslides
   basics about, 92
   facts and figures, 6, 93
   safety information, 92-96
   types of, 93

B

baking soda
   paste, using for first aid treatment, 27, 29, 40, 61
   uses for, 68
biological agents, safety information, 129-131
bites
   animals or humans, first aid for, 26
   snakes, first aid for, 29-30
bites and stings
   insects, first aid for, 27-28
   marine animals, first aid for, 28-29
   scorpions and spiders, first aid for, 30-31
bleeding, controlling, 32-33
body parts, severed or amputated, emergency measures, 33
bomb threats, 130-131
bones, broken or fractured, first aid treatment, 36-37
building explosions, safety information, 131
burns, first aid treatment, 38-40
   chemical, 39
   electrical, 39-40
   fire or hot liquids, 38-39
   sunburn, 40

C

P

pain relief aids, 27-28, 29, 31, 61, 68-69
  for burns, 40
personal hygiene items, for disaster supplies kit, 75-76
personal information, checklist form, 10-11
pets
  emergency preparedness checklist, 15
  and emergency shelters, 146
plants, poisonous
  first aid treatment when exposed to, 60-61
  illustrations of, 62-63
poison
  ivy; oak; sumac, 60-63
poisonings, first aid treatment when, 59-61
  absorbed through skin, 59
  exposed to poisonous plant, 60-61
  inhaled, 59-60
  swallowed, 64
provincial emergency measures organizations, 166-167

R

radiation exposure from nuclear power plants,
  radioactive iodine, 124-125
  safety information, 124-128
rescue breathing. *See* mouth-to-mouth resuscitation
resources, 180-186

S

SAFE GUARD, emergency preparedness program, 90, 166, 171-172
sanitation
  disposal of human waste in disaster situation, 82
  disaster supplies kit, 75-76
scorpion stings, first aid treatment for, 30-31
seizures, first aid treatment for, 46
shelters, living in short-term following a disaster, 146
shock, first aid treatment for, 65
SIDS (Sudden Infant Death Syndrome)
  Alliance (organization), x, xii-xiii
  facts and information, xi
smoke detectors, 88, 106
snake bites, first aid treatment for, 29-30
spider bites, first aid treatment for, 30-31

spine injuries, first aid treatment for, 51
state emergency management agencies, 159-162
stroke, first aid treatment for, 66
Sudden Infant Death Syndrome. *See* SIDS
sunburn, first aid treatment for, 40
syrup of ipecac, uses for, 64, 69

T
tea tree oil, for pain relief, 31
terrorism
    biological agents, safety information, 129-130
    bomb threats, safety information, 130-131
    building explosions, 131
    chemical agents, safety information, 129-130
    facts and figures, 6, 129
    sample county emergency preparedness outline, 173-179
    weapons of mass destruction (WMD), 126, 130, 173-179
thunderstorms. *See also* lightning
    facts and figures, 6, 132
    safety information, 132-133
tools and supplies, for disaster supplies kit, 74-75
tornadoes
    facts and figures, 6, 134
    safety information, 134-136
    trailer homes, safety tips, 84, 135
tsunamis
    facts and figures, 7, 137
    safety information, 101, 137-139
    Web sites, 186
typhoons, 120. *See also* hurricanes
    facts and figures, 5

U-V-W
urine, first aid uses for, 28, 29
vinegar, first aid uses for, 40, 69
volcanoes
    facts and figures, 17, 140
    safety information, 141-142
volunteers, offering help for disaster relief, 153-154
water
    purifying for drinking, 81
    for disaster supplies kit, 73